Notification concerning Planned Measures on Shared Watercourses

AF714437

International Water Law

Editor-in-Chief

Salman M. A. Salman (*IWRA*)

Associate Editors

Laurence Boisson de Chazournes (*University of Geneva*)
Lilian del Castillo-Laborde (*University of Buenos Aires*)
Gabriel Eckstein (*Texas A&M University*)
Makane Moise Mbengue (*University of Geneva*)
Alistair Rieu-Clarke (*University of Dundee*)
Kishor Uprety (*International Lawyer and Researcher*)

Volumes published in this Brill Research Perspective are listed at *brill.com/rpwl*

Notification concerning Planned Measures on Shared Watercourses

Synergies between the Watercourses Convention and the World Bank Policies and Practice

By

Salman M. A. Salman

BRILL

LEIDEN | BOSTON

This paperback book edition is simultaneously published as Volume 4 (2) 2019 in *International Water Law*, DOI:10.1163/23529369-12340014.

Library of Congress Control Number: 2019942844

Typeface for the Latin, Greek, and Cyrillic scripts: "Brill". See and download: brill.com/brill-typeface.

ISBN 978-90-04-40744-2 (paperback)
ISBN 978-90-04-40745-9 (e-book)

Copyright 2019 by Salman M. A. Salman. Published by Koninklijke Brill NV, Leiden, The Netherlands. Koninklijke Brill NV incorporates the imprints Brill, Brill Hes & De Graaf, Brill Nijhoff, Brill Rodopi, Brill Sense, Hotei Publishing, mentis Verlag, Verlag Ferdinand Schöningh and Wilhelm Fink Verlag. Koninklijke Brill NV reserves the right to protect the publication against unauthorized use and to authorize dissemination by means of offprints, legitimate photocopies, microform editions, reprints, translations, and secondary information sources, such as abstracting and indexing services including databases. Requests for commercial re-use, use of parts of the publication, and/or translations must be addressed to Koninklijke Brill NV.

This book is printed on acid-free paper and produced in a sustainable manner.

To the memory of Dr. Raj Krishna (1933–2005); in recognition of his steadfast intellectual efforts in aligning the World Bank policies and practice for projects on shared watercourses with the principles of international water law.

Contents

Acknowledgements

I would like to extend my sincere thanks and appreciation to Professor Laurence Boisson de Chazournes for undertaking and handling in a very efficient and diligent manner the responsibilities of "Interim Editor-in-Chief" for this monograph. My thanks and appreciation are also due to the anonymous reviewers, as well as the members of the Editorial Board of *Brill Research Perspectives in International Water Law*, for overseeing the review process, and for the helpful and constructive comments on the monograph.

Notification concerning Planned Measures on Shared Watercourses

Synergies between the Watercourses Convention and the World Bank Policies and Practice

Salman M. A. Salman
Fellow, International Water Resources Association (IWRA)
salmanmasalman@gmail.com

Abstract

Notification of co-riparian states of planned measures on shared watercourses has been widely accepted as an established principle of international water law, and is codified and elaborated in the United Nations Watercourses Convention. However, despite this wide acceptance, issues have arisen in operationalizing notification, and in dealing with the different types of responses that may ensue following notification. The World Bank has been financing projects on international watercourses since its inception in the late 1940s, and has built an extensive wealth of policies and experience in this field. This monograph discusses the historical and legal foundations of notification under international law, analyses the policies and implementation experience of the World Bank thereon, and identifies comparators and synergies between the provisions of the Watercourses Convention and the Bank policies and practice.

Keywords

notification – riparian states – shared watercourses – Watercourses Convention – World Bank Policies

Part 1: Introduction

Notification of co-riparian states of planned measures on shared watercourses that may result in significant adverse effects has been widely accepted as one of the established principles of international water law. The emergence and acceptance of notification are a "culmination of a long process of its recognition

© SALMAN M. A. SALMAN, 2019 | DOI:10.1163/9789004407459_002

as a principle of international law that is critically important in the environmental area."[1] Indeed, this wide acceptance of notification has been codified and elaborated by the 1997 United Nations Convention on the Law of the Non-Navigational Uses of International Watercourses (Watercourses Convention).[2] The Convention includes one separate part (Part III – Planned Measures), with nine articles, on notification.

The duty to notify other states of activities that may affect them stems from good faith, good neighbourliness, and reciprocity.[3] It is an extension of the general obligation under international law to cooperate and to exchange data and information on shared watercourses. Such cooperation is no doubt the *sine qua non* for the equitable, sustainable, and efficient utilization and protection of international watercourses.[4] Moreover, notification is the only effective way for knowing about and judging the unilateral activities by one or more of the riparians that may affect other riparian states and the shared watercourse itself.

Professor Charles Bourne distinguished between three kinds of notice by a state to a co-basin state, or to co-basin states:

> First, there is the notice that may be given by a state that is proposing to utilize the waters of a drainage basin; then there is the notice that may be given by a state that is aware of a situation in its territory, not voluntarily created by it, which may cause injury to co-basin states; and, finally, there is the notice that may be given by a state to warn co-basin states that their acts may affect its present or future rights or interests in the resources of the drainage basin.[5]

---

1 L. Boisson de Chazournes & K. Sangbana, *'Principle 19: Notification and Consultation on Activities with Transboundary Impact'*, in J. E. Viñuales (ed.), *The Rio Declaration on Environment and Development: A Commentary* (Oxford: Oxford University Press, 2015) 493–507, at 494.

2 *See* S. M. A. Salman, *'Entry into Force of the UN Watercourses Convention – Why Should It Matter?'*, 31:1 International Journal of Water Resources Development (2015) 4–16. As will be discussed later, the Convention was adopted by the United Nations General Assembly (UNGA) on 21 May 1997 and entered into force on 17 August 2014.

3 M. M. Farrajota, *'Notification and Consultation in the Law Applicable to International Watercourses'*, in L. Boisson de Chazournes & S. M. A. Salman (eds.), *Water Resources and International Law* (The Hague Academy of International Law, 2005), at 281.

4 *See* generally, C. Leb, *Cooperation in the Law of Transboundary Water Resources* (Cambridge: Cambridge University Press, 2013).

5 P. Wouters, ed., *International Water Law, Selected Writings of Professor Charles Bourne* (Kluwer Law International, 1997) at 83.

Thus, Professor Bourne has aptly extended and expanded application of the notification requirement to include not only projects and programs by one riparian state, but also to encompass notification for involuntary situations, as well as notification to another riparian state regarding its failure to notify.

It should be added that the notification requirement and its details have recently become the focus of attention and developments in a number of global fora, which have energized the debate on notification. This debate has also dealt with the details of operationalization of notification, including the different types of responses to notification and the manner for dealing with them, particularly with regards to objections following notification.

A major development in the field of notification is the decision of the International Court of Justice (ICJ) in 2010 in the *Pulp Mills* case.[6] That decision has gone beyond endorsing the notification requirement under the Statute of the River Uruguay, concluded by Argentina and Uruguay in 1975.[7] Indeed, the ICJ considered notification as a *sine qua non* of cooperation, in addition to being a vital method for protecting the shared watercourse. The ICJ stated in this regard that it

> considers that the procedural obligations of informing, notifying and negotiating constitute an appropriate means, accepted by the Parties, of achieving the objective which they set themselves in Article 1 of the 1975 Statute. These obligations are all the more vital when a shared resource is at issue, as in the case of the River Uruguay, which can only be protected through close and continuous co-operation between the riparian States.[8]

This clear and unequivocal endorsement of notification has no doubt highlighted and strengthened both the procedural and substantive normative contents of notification, as the ICJ itself has stipulated. It has also reconfirmed the strong linkages between notification and cooperation.

In that same year, 2010, negotiations over the Nile River Basin Cooperative Framework Agreement (CFA)[9] among the Nile Basin countries collapsed after more than ten years of facilitation by the World Bank and some other donors. The collapse resulted from insistence by Egypt and Sudan on inclusion of a

---

6 International Court of Justice (ICJ), *Case concerning Pulp Mills on the River Uruguay* (*Argentina v. Uruguay*), Judgement, 20 April 2010.

7 Salto, 25 February 1975, 1295 U. N. T. S. 331 (1982).

8 *Pulp Mills* case, *supra* note 6, para. 81.

9 The Agreement on the Nile River Basin Cooperative Framework, Entebbe, 14 May 2010 (CFA) is available at: http://www.nilebasin.org/images/docs/CFA%20-%20English%20%20FrenchVersion.pdf.

specific reference in the CFA to what they consider as their 'acquired rights' over the Nile waters, claiming that such rights represent their vital and absolute 'water security' which, they have insisted, is non-negotiable.[10] They based such rights on their claim to the validity of two contested Nile treaties, one concluded in 1902,[11] and the other in 1929,[12] which, they argue, establish and confirm such rights.[13] The other Nile riparians have rejected vehemently the inclusion of such a reference in the CFA and contested the validity of these two Nile treaties. These riparians have kept arguing for equitable and reasonable utilization of the Nile waters among all the Nile riparian states, with no preferential treatment whatsoever for one riparian over the others.

Egypt and Sudan also insist on inclusion in the CFA of provisions on notification similar to those of the UN Watercourses Convention.[14] The CFA includes provisions on exchange of data and information,[15] but none on notification.

---

10 *See* D. Mekonnen, *'The Nile Basin Cooperative Framework Agreement Negotiations and the Adoption of a "Water Security" Paradigm: Flight into Obscurity or a Logical Cul-de-sac?'* 21:2 European Journal of International Law (2010) 421–440. For a detailed discussion of the concept of water security as a political and not a legal one, *see* S. M. A. Salman & K. Uprety, *'Shared Watercourses and Water Security in South Asia – Challenges of Negotiating and Enforcing Treaties'*, 3:3 International Water Law (2018).

11 *See* Treaty between Ethiopia and the United Kingdom relative to the frontiers between the Anglo-Egyptian Sudan, Ethiopia, and Eritrea, Adis Ababa, 15 May 1902), Treaty Series 016/1902: Cd. 1370.

12 *See* Exchange of Notes between Great Britain and Northern Ireland and Egypt in Regard to the Use of the Waters of the River Nile for Irrigation Purposes, Cairo, 7 May 1929, Treaty Series 017/1929: Cmd 3348.

13 Egypt claims to have succeeded to the 1902 treaty between Britain and Ethiopia, and alleges further that the treaty gives it veto power over projects on the Nile in Ethiopia, a claim rejected totally by Ethiopia. Egypt also claims that the 1929 treaty between Britain (on behalf of its colonies of Kenya, Tanganyika, Uganda, and Sudan) and Egypt gives it veto power over projects on the Nile in these British colonies. In contrast, Kenya, Tanganyika (now Tanzania), and Uganda claim that they are no longer bound by the agreement. For a thorough discussion of these agreements and issues, *see* S. M. A. Salman, *'The Nile River Basin and its Changing Legal Contours'*, in S. McCaffrey, C. Leb & R. T. Denoon (eds.), *Research Handbook on International Water Law* (Cheltenham: Edward Elgar, 2019) 379–396; *see also* Z. Yihdego, *'The Fairness Dilemma in Sharing the Nile Waters: What Lessons from the Grand Ethiopian Renaissance Dam?'*, 2:2 International Water Law (2017).

14 It is interesting to note that neither Egypt nor Sudan is a party to the UN Watercourses Convention, despite their reliance on the Convention. Indeed, none of the Nile Basin countries is a party to the Convention. Kenya and Sudan voted for the Convention during the UN General Assembly meeting on 21 May 1997, while Burundi voted against the Convention (together with China and Turkey). Egypt, Ethiopia, Rwanda, and Tanzania abstained, each for its own reasons. The Democratic Republic of Congo, Eritrea, and Uganda did not participate in the vote. *See* S. M. A. Salman, *'The Nile Basin Cooperative Framework Agreement: A Peacefully Unfolding African Spring?'*, 38:1 Water International (2013) 17–29.

15 Article 7 of the CFA (*supra* note 9) states: "In pursuance of their cooperation concerning the use, development and protection of the Nile River Basin and its water resources,

The other riparians have strongly opposed the inclusion of provisions on, or even a reference to, notification, in the CFA. They argue that the objective of Egypt and Sudan is to give themselves the opportunity to claim, through the reply to notification, the validity of these two contested treaties. Six Nile riparian states have thus far signed the CFA, and three of them have ratified it, but Egypt and Sudan continue to vehemently oppose the CFA. The CFA needs six instruments of ratification/accession to enter into force.[16]

The current thinking amongst some Nile observers for breaking the impasse over the CFA is for Egypt and Sudan to drop their claims of 'acquired rights' over the Nile waters, and consequently to drop the reference to water security in the CFA, and for the other riparians to agree on the inclusion of provisions on notification in the CFA, similar to those of the Watercourses Convention.[17]

Another development that has highlighted the concept of notification and energized the debate thereon relates to the gradual and wide acknowledgement that harm, under international water law, is actually a two-way matter with regards to the issue of quantitative allocation of the waters of shared rivers. Just as upstream riparians can harm downstream ones through storage, diversion, and use of the waters of shared rivers, downstream riparians can also harm upstream riparians by foreclosing their future uses of the shared waters through the prior use of and the claiming of rights to such water, and invoking the no harm obligation.[18] Based on this theory, which will be discussed in part 3 of this monograph, notification for projects that may have significant adverse effects is required from all, and to all, the riparians of the shared watercourse. The wider acceptance of the concept of foreclosure of future uses has started to correct the mistaken notion that notification is only required for downstream riparians because harm travels with the flow of the waters of the shared river. It is now widely agreed that notification is required from all and to all the riparians of the shared watercourse.

Nile Basin States shall on a regular basis exchange readily available and relevant data and information on existing measures and on the condition of water resources of the Basin, where possible in a form that facilitates its utilization by the States to which it is communicated."

16 *See* Salman, *The Nile Basin Cooperative Framework Agreement, supra* note 14, at 22.

17 S. M. A. Salman, *'The Nile Basin Cooperative Framework Agreement: The Impasse is Breakable!'*, available at: https://www.internationalwaterlaw.org/blog/2017/06/19/the-nile-basin-cooperative-framework-agreement-the-impasse-is-breakable/.

18 For a detailed analysis of this matter, *see* Salman M. A. Salman, *'The Obligation not to Cause Significant Harm'*, in L. Boisson de Chazournes et al (eds.), *The UN Convention on the Law of the Non-Navigational Uses of International Watercourse: A Commentary* (Oxford: Oxford University Press, 2018), 95–122, at 115; *see also* S. M. A. Salman, *'Downstream Riparians Can also Harm Upstream Riparians: The Concept of Foreclosure of Future Uses'*, 35:4 *Water International* (2010) 350–364, at 350.

The fourth development in the realm of notification relates to the discussion and attempts of the World Bank,[19] which started in 2005 the process of amending the provisions on notification in the Bank Policy for "Projects on International Waterways."[20] The purpose of the proposed amendment is to align the Bank Policy with the provisions of the Watercourses Convention with regards to the threshold for notification.[21] Indeed, the World Bank has one of the pioneering and elaborate policies, and the only practical experience, among international organizations in the field of international water law generally, and on notification in particular. The Policy has evolved gradually during the long years of the practical experience of the Bank in this field, and as a result of the extensive and challenging experience gained from the large number of projects on international waterways that the Bank has financed since the late 1940s. The Policy, as discussed below in this monograph, does not establish a threshold for notification of other riparians of projects on international waterways. It requires notification as a general rule for all projects on international waterways, and sets forth three exceptions to the notification

---

19 A distinction needs to be made at the outset between the 'International Bank for Reconstruction and Development – IBRD', 'The World Bank', and 'The World Bank Group.' The term 'The World Bank' refers to both IBRD and the International Development Association (IDA). IBRD was established in 1944 and started its operations in 1946. IBRD operations are concentrated in middle-income countries and creditworthy poor countries, and its funding is called 'loans'. IDA was established in 1960 to provide interest-free credits to its poorest member countries, and its funding is called 'credits'. The wider term, The World Bank Group (WBG), includes, in addition to IBRD and IDA, the International Finance Corporation (IFC), the Multilateral Investment Guarantee Agency (MIGA), and the International Centre for Settlement of Investment Disputes (ICSID). For more details on each of those institutions, *see* www.worldbank.org. For the articles of agreement of each of these institutions, *see:* http://web.worldbank.org/WBSITE/EXTERNAL/EXTABOUTUS/ORGANIZATION/BODEXT/0,,contentMDK:50004943~menuPK:64020045~pagePK:64020054~piPK:64020408~theSitePK:278036,00.html.

20 It should be added here that the International Finance Corporation (IFC, *see id.,*) also has a Policy for Projects on International Waterways that is similar to the World Bank policy; it is even numbered OP 7.50. The IFC Policy is available at: https://www.ifc.org/wps/wcm/connect/f3d5c40048855a708604d66a6515bb18/OP750_IntlWaterways.pdf?MOD=AJPERES. Since the IFC Policy is similar to the World Bank Policy, and cannot be amended without the Bank Policy itself being amended first, reference is made throughout this monograph to the "World Bank Policy" in a generic sense to include both the World Bank and the IFC policies as they are one and the same policy.

21 The process of amending the Policy for Projects on International Waterways to establish a threshold for notification started in 2005 and was handled by a committee representing different units within the Bank. The author of this monograph, in his capacity as the World Bank Water Law Advisor at that time and until his retirement in 2009, was the focal point of that committee and the process.

requirement. This stands in contrast to the Watercourses Convention, which requires notification for projects that may result in 'significant adverse effect' on other riparians.

The debate within the Bank on its policy for projects on international waterways that commenced in 2005 centred on whether the Bank should align its policy with the Watercourses Convention and most other regional instruments and establish a threshold for notification, or whether it should continue to follow its long-standing policy and practice in this field, which sets no threshold for notification. As may be expected, the Bank member countries themselves, like the World Bank staff and management, are divided on this issue between those arguing for the alignment and the amendment of the policy, and those demanding that the policy stays as is. It remains to be seen if and how this matter will eventually resolve itself.

It is interesting to note that the Asian Infrastructure Investment Bank (AIIB), which started its operations in 2016,[22] adopted in March 2017 a series of operational policies, including the "Operational Policy on International Relations." Section 3 of the Operational Policy deals with international waterways. This section is based largely on the World Bank Policy for Projects on International Waterways, and included the proposed revisions to the Bank Policy to establish a threshold for notification, which have not yet been approved by the World Bank. Paragraph 3.3(c)(i) of the AIIB Policy states that notification is not required for "[p]Projects that are expected to have minimal or no effect on any of the other riparians."[23] These are the same words for the World Bank proposed amendment to its Policy for Projects on International Waterways.

Aside from the AIIB, whose Operational Policy dealing with projects on international waterways is quite recent, and with no substantive implementation experience thus far, no other international or regional financial institution has an explicit policy for projects on international waterways. However, these institutions usually avoid financing projects on shared watercourses that may

22 The Asian Infrastructure Investment Bank (AIIB) is a development bank established in 2016 with the objective of improving economic and social conditions in Asia. AIIB headquarters are in Beijing. For more information about AIIB, *see* https://www.aiib.org/en/index.html.

23 The AIIB "Operational Policy on International Relations" is available at: https://www.aiib.org/en/policies-strategies/_download/operational-policy-on-international-relations/operational-policy-on-international-relations.pdf. It should be pointed out that a number of consultants/experts who helped with preparation of the AIIB operational policies are former World Bank staff. For this reason, the AIIB policies are based largely on the World Bank policies. Indeed, the choice of the term "international waterways" by AIIB is noteworthy.

result in harm to one or more of the riparians, or in disputes among them. In other projects with minimal or no harm, senior management of most of these institutions usually consult with the executive directors representing the affected riparians before proceeding with projects on international waterways.[24]

It should be added here that the World Bank approved in August 2016 a new Environmental and Social Framework (ESF),[25] which replaced the earlier set of policies called "the safeguard policies.[26] The Bank Policy for Projects on International Waterways had been one of these safeguard policies. However, the new revised ESF and accompanying Environmental and Social Standards (ESS) do not include the Bank Policy for Projects on International Waterways which, together with the Policy on Disputed Areas, were left unchanged.[27]

---

24 This information is based on interviews with legal staff from the Asian Development Bank (AsDB), the African Development Bank (AfDB), as well as the International Fund for Agricultural Development (IFAD). The author of this monograph served as a legal officer with IFAD, and participated in the consultations with executive directors representing riparian states regarding the few projects where the issue of the effects of projects on shared watercourses arose. Some of these projects were co-financed with either the AsDB, or the AfDB.

25 *See 'World Bank Board Approves New Environmental and Social Framework'* World Bank Press Release (4 August 2016), available at: http://www.worldbank.org/en/news/press-release/2016/08/04/world-bank-board-approves-new-environmental-and-social-framework.

26 The safeguard policies included the ten policies on environmental assessment, natural habitats, forestry, pest management, safety of dams, cultural property, indigenous peoples, involuntary resettlement, disputed areas, and projects on international waterways. *See 'Former Environmental and Social Safeguards and Supporting Materials'* available at: http://www.ifc.org/safeguards. The World Bank carved out these ten policies from among the large number of its operational policies and named them the "safeguard policies." Compliance by Bank staff with all the operational policies, particularly the safeguard policies, is mandatory. Moreover, the World Bank established the Inspection Panel as an independent accountability mechanism to address non-compliance with any of its operational policies. For more details on the Inspection Panel, *see* https://www.inspectionpanel.org/.

27 The ten new Environmental and Social Standards that have replaced the first eight safeguard policies are: Assessment and Management of Environmental and Social Risks and Impacts; Labor and Working Conditions; Resource Efficiency and Pollution Prevention and Management; Community Health and Safety; Land Acquisition, Restriction on Land Use and Involuntary Resettlement; Biodiversity Conservation and Sustainable Management of Living Natural Resources; Indigenous Peoples/ Sub-Saharan African Historically Underserved Traditional and Local Communities; Cultural Heritage; Financial Intermediaries; and Stakeholder Engagement and Information Disclosure. For a detailed discussion of the ESF and the new Environmental and Social Standards, *see* The World Bank, *The World Bank Environmental and Social Framework* (Washington, DC: The World Bank, 2017).

It seems that the extensive work and consultations on the ESF sidelined the discussions on the amendments to the Bank Policy for Projects on International Waterways to align it with the Watercourses Convention. The ESF, launched on 1 October 2018, and the ESS have, as of that date, replaced the other eight Bank safeguard policies, as well as the Bank Policy on Disclosure of Information.[28] It remains to be seen how the process of amending the International Waterways Policy, which has now been delinked from the ESF and ESS, will proceed and unravel. Thus, the notification process and its operationalization continue to occupy a large space of the current global debate on international water law, and these four developments, among others, have energized this debate.

The purpose of this monograph is to trace the historical and legal origins of the notification requirement, including those of the World Bank policies, analyse the provisions of the Watercourses Convention as well as those of the Bank policies and Bank practice, and identify the main areas of congruence and difference between them. The monograph will also discern the synergies between the provisions of the Watercourses Convention and the policies and practice of the World Bank on notification, and draw some lessons for international water law therefrom.

Part 2: Evolution of the Notification Requirement

As indicated above, the duty to notify other states of activities on shared watercourses that may affect them stems from good faith, good neighbourliness, and reciprocity. Consequently, a number of regional treaties, soft law instruments, and judicial and arbitral decisions have addressed the issue of notification, and contributed to the evolution of the current rules and practice that have been largely codified in the Watercourses Convention.

One of the early instruments to address the notification requirement is the Montevideo Declaration issued by the Seventh International Conference of American States in 1933. Paragraph 7 of the Declaration requires that:

> [t]he works which a state plans to perform in international waters shall be previously announced to the other riparian or co-jurisdictional states. The announcement shall be accompanied by the necessary technical

28 *See 'As the World Bank is poised to launch its new framework of environmental and social policies, borrowing countries are preparing to implement it',* The World Bank (6 July 2018), available at: https://www.worldbank.org/en/news/feature/2018/07/06/borrowing-countries-prepare-for-esf-launch.

> documentation in order that the other interested states may judge the scope of such works, and by the name of the technical expert or experts who are to deal, if necessary, with the international side of the matter.[29]

Thus, the Montevideo Declaration addressed both the procedural requirement of notification, and its substantive content as well – attaching the necessary technical documentation to the notification.

A quarter of a century later, the notification requirement was strengthened and elaborated by the decision of the arbitral tribunal in the *Lake Lanoux* case.[30] The arbitration dealt with the proposed use by the French government of the waters of Lake Lanoux for carrying out certain hydro-electric works. The Lake is fed by some streams originating and flowing through French territory. Its waters emerge by the Font-Vive stream that forms one of the headwaters of the River Carol, which flows into Spain, where it joins the River Segre. Spain opposed the use of the waters of Lake Lanoux by France, claiming adverse effects as a result of such use. While the tribunal decided that the works did not constitute infringement of Spain's rights, it also ruled that France was entitled to use the waters of Lake Lanoux, but could not ignore Spain's interests, and that Spain was entitled to demand that Spanish rights be respected, and its interests be taken into account.

On the issue of notification, the arbitral tribunal amply clarified the matter when it explicitly stated that:

> [a] state wishing to do that which will affect an international watercourse cannot decide whether another State's interest will be affected; the other state is the sole judge of that and has the right to information on the proposals.[31]

Indeed, the tribunal considered notification and the accompanying information as a right of the other riparian states, which correspondingly means it is the duty of the state planning the measures on the shared watercourse to notify other riparian states. However, the tribunal clarified that this right to notification does not carry with it veto power over the proposed activity, only

---

29 Paragraph 6 of the Montevideo Declaration deals with navigation and requires that riparian states not carry out any works that may injure free navigation and communicate to the other riparian states the studies on any planned works. For the full text of the Declaration, *see* 28 American Journal of International Law, supp. (1934), at 59.

30 *Lake Lanoux Arbitration (France v. Spain)*, 24 I.L.R. 101 (1957); B. MacChesney, '*Lake Lanoux Case (France-Spain)*', 53:1 American Journal of International Law (1959) 156–171.

31 *Id.*

the right to object. The statement by the Lake Lanoux tribunal on "whether another State's interests will be affected" is a reference to the obligation against causing harm that has been explicitly included in the relevant provisions of the UN Watercourses Convention, as will be discussed below.

Among the early treaties that addressed the issue of notification is the Indus Waters Treaty concluded between India and Pakistan in 1960.[32] The Treaty divided the six rivers of the Indus River System between the two countries.[33] Nevertheless the Treaty requires the state that plans to construct engineering works that would cause interference with the waters of any of the rivers of the Indus Basin, and which in its opinion would affect the other party materially, to notify the other party of its plans.[34] The notifying state is required to supply the other state with the available data relating to the proposed works to enable that state to inform itself of the nature, magnitude, and effect of the works.[35]

The Indus Waters Treaty goes on to state: "If a work would cause interference with the waters of any of the rivers but would not, in the opinion of the Party planning it, affect the other Party materially, nevertheless the Party planning the work shall, on request, supply the other Party with such data regarding the

32 *The Indus Waters Treaty*, India-Pakistan, 19 September 1960, 419 U.N.T.S. 126 (1962). The Treaty was signed by Mr. Jawaharlal Nehru, Prime Minister of India, and Field Marshal Mohammad Ayub Khan, President of Pakistan. Mr. W. A. B. Iliff signed on behalf of the World Bank for certain articles and annexures specified in the Treaty. For a detailed analysis of the Indus Waters Treaty, *see* S. M. A. Salman & K. Uprety, *Conflict and Cooperation on South Asia's International Rivers: A Legal Perspective* (The Hague: Kluwer Law International, 2003; Washington, DC: World Bank, 2003).

33 The main features of the Indus Waters Treaty, *id.*, include (i) allocation of the three Eastern Rivers of the Indus System (Ravi, Sutlej and Beas) to India; (ii) allocation of the three Western Rivers (Indus, Jhelum and Chenab) to Pakistan; (iii) construction of replacement works by Pakistan to meet its Eastern Rivers needs from the Western Rivers; (iv) incorporation of safeguards in the Treaty to ensure unrestricted flow of the waters in the Western Rivers to Pakistan, subject to some uses by India; (v) regular exchange of flow-data of rivers, canals, and streams between the parties; and (vi) establishment of a Permanent Indus Commission to oversee implementation of the Treaty.

34 Indus Waters Treaty, *id.*, art. VII(2).

35 Notification and exchange of data and information between the two countries are carried out mainly through the Permanent Indus Commission which consists of one commissioner from each of the two countries. The Commission is also entrusted with the responsibility of trying to resolve any question that may arise between the two parties regarding interpretation or application of the Indus Waters Treaty. If the Commission fails to resolve any such question, then the question becomes a difference, and is referred to a Neutral Expert (*see* Annexure F of the Treaty). Moreover, certain issues are classified as disputes and can be referred for resolution to a Court of Arbitration (see Annexure G of the Treaty). *See* also Salman & Uprety, *Shared Watercourses, supra* note 10.

nature, magnitude and effect, if any, of the work as may be available."[36] This is basically a clear endorsement of the Lake Lanoux judgment that the decision on the effects of the planned works is not left solely for the planning state; rather, it is for the other riparian states to evaluate and judge. In addition to the notification requirement, the Indus Waters Treaty includes detailed requirements on regular exchange of data and information between the two parties.[37]

Mention should also be made in this connection to the contribution of two scholarly non-governmental organizations – the Institute of International Law (IIL)[38] and the International Law Association (ILA)[39] – in the field of international water law generally, and on notification in particular. The IIL issued its first resolution on shared watercourses, the Madrid Declaration, in 1911.[40] The crux of the Declaration is the right of the state to use the waters of an international watercourse in its territory, but only in such a manner as not to cause appreciable harm to other riparians. Thus, the Madrid Declaration laid down the basis for the prohibition of causing appreciable harm to other riparians. Moreover, the Declaration required the consent of the other riparians, although it did not include explicit provisions on notification.

---

36 Indus Waters Treaty, supra note 32, art. VII(2). Annexure D of the Treaty deals with plants and construction of river works for the generation of hydroelectric power by India on the Western Rivers allocated to Pakistan, and the provision of information on such plants and works by India to Pakistan, and Pakistan's response. Similar provisions are also included in Annexure E with regard to storage of waters by India on the Western Rivers; *see* Salman & Uprety, *Cooperation and Conflict, supra* note 32.

37 The Treaty, *id.*, specifies a wide range of data that should be transmitted monthly to one another by each party, including (a) daily (or as observed or estimated less frequently) gauge and discharge data relating to flow of the rivers at all observation sites; (b) daily extractions for or releases from reservoirs; (c) daily withdrawals at the heads of all canals operated by governments, including link canals; (d) daily escapages from all canals, including link canals; and (e) daily deliveries from link canals. Article VI(2) of the Treaty further states that other available data related to any provision of the Treaty should be supplied to the other party, and vice versa, on request. *See* also Salman & Uprety, *supra* note 32. For other regional and bilateral agreements that address the issue of notification, *see* L. Boisson de Chazournes, *Freshwater and International Law: The Interplay between Universal, Regional and Basin Perspectives* (Paris: UNESCO, 2009).

38 The Institute of International Law (IIL) was established in 1873 and consists of selected invited members. The IIL objective "is to promote the progress of international law." *'About the Institute'*, IIL, available at: http://www.idi-iil.org/en/a-propos/.

39 The International Law Association (ILA) was also founded in 1873. However, membership of the ILA is open to all international lawyers, and is not by invitation, as is the case with the IIL. The objectives of the Association are "the study, clarification and development of international law". *'About Us'*, ILA, available at: http://www.ila-hq.org/.

40 *'International Regulations Regarding the Use of International Watercourses for Purposes Other than Navigation'*, 24 Annuaire de l'Institut de Droit International 365 (1911).

It would take 50 years before the IIL would adopt another resolution on international waters, the Salzburg Resolution issued in 1961.[41] The Resolution applied to the utilization of waters which form part of a watercourse or hydrographic basin that extends over the territory of two or more states.[42] The Resolution stated that if the riparian states are in disagreement over the scope of their rights of utilization of the shared watercourse, settlement will take place on the basis of equity, taking particular account of their respective needs, as well as of other pertinent circumstances.

The Salzburg Resolution addressed notification when it confirmed the right of the riparian states to undertake works or utilization of the waters of a watercourse or hydrographic basin that may seriously affect the possibility of utilization of the same waters by other riparian states. However, such works can only be undertaken after previous notice is provided to the interested states.[43] In case an objection is made, the Resolution requires the riparian states to enter into negotiations with a view to reaching an agreement within a reasonable period of time. During the negotiations, every state must, in conformity with the principle of good faith, refrain from undertaking the works or utilization that are the object of the dispute, or from taking any other measures that might aggravate the dispute or render agreement more difficult. If the states fail to reach agreement within a reasonable time, the Resolution recommends that they submit the question to judicial settlement or arbitration.[44] Thus, the Salzburg Resolution addressed and corrected the various shortcomings and rigidity of the Madrid Declaration regarding the need for the consent of the notified state or states.

The ILA started working on shared watercourses in 1954, and issued a few statements and resolutions before adopting the famous Helsinki Rules on the Uses of the Waters of International Rivers in 1966.[45] The Rules incorporated and elaborated the previous statements and resolutions adopted successively at Dubrovnik, New York, and Tokyo.[46] Although the title of the Rules refers to

41 *'Resolution on the Utilization of Non-Maritime International Waters (Except for Navigation), adopted by the Institute of International Law at its Session at Salzburg (Salzburg Resolution), 11 September 1961'*, 49 Annuaire de l'Institut de Droit International 370 (1961); *see also* 56 American Journal of International Law 737 (1962).

42 *Id.*, art. 1.

43 *Id.*, art. 5.

44 *Id.*, arts. 5 and 6.

45 International Law Association, *Report of the Fifty-Second Conference* (Helsinki, 1966) 486 [hereinafter the Helsinki Rules].

46 For a detailed account of the work of the ILA in this field, *see* C. Bourne, *'The International Law Association's Contribution to International Water Resources Law'*, 36 *Natural Resources Journal* (1996) 155–216; *see also* S. Bogdanovic, *International Law of Water*

international rivers only, Article 1 states that the Rules are applicable to the use of the waters of an international drainage basin. Such a drainage basin is defined as "a geographical area extending over two or more States determined by the watershed limits of the system of waters, including surface and underground waters, flowing into a common terminus."[47]

The Helsinki Rules deal extensively with the principle of reasonable and equitable utilization and have established the principle as the guiding rule of the work of the ILA, as well as of international water law. The Rules devote a separate chapter to procedures, not only for settlement, but also for the prevention of disputes. These procedures include both the exchange of data and information on the drainage basin between the riparian states, as well as notification.

With regards to notification, Article XXIX of the Helsinki Rules requires a state, regardless of its location in a drainage basin, to furnish to any other basin state, the interests of which may be substantially affected, notice of any proposed construction or installation which would alter the regime of the basin in a way that might give rise to a dispute. The notice should include such essential facts as would permit the recipient to make an assessment of the probable effect of the proposed alteration. The notifying state should give the recipient a reasonable period of time to study and assess the probable effect of the proposed construction or installation and to submit its views thereon to the notifying state. In case of a dispute between these states as to their legal rights or other interests, they should seek a solution by negotiation.

It should be added that the Helsinki Rules were regarded, soon after their issuance, as the most authoritative set of rules for regulating the use and protection of international watercourses. As noted by Professor Bourne, the Helsinki Rules were soon accepted by the international community as customary international law.[48] Indeed, the Rules continued to be, until the adoption of the Watercourses Convention in 1997, the most widely quoted and relied upon set of rules on international water law.

Notification also forms an important part of a number of soft law instruments. Building on previous work, particularly the 1966 Helsinki Rules, the United Nations Environmental Programme (UNEP) issued in 1978 the Environmental Law Guidelines and Principles on Shared Natural Resources. Principle 6 (1) of the Guidelines states:

Resources: Contribution of the International Law Association (Kluwer Law International, 2001); S. Bogdanovic, *'The International Law Association Helsinki Rules: Contribution to International Water Law'*, 3:4 International Water Law (2018).

47 Helsinki Rules, *supra* note 45, art. II.

48 Bourne, *supra* note 46, at 215.

> It is necessary for every State sharing a natural resource with one or more other States: (a) to notify in advance the other State or States of the pertinent details of plans to initiate, or make change in, the conservation or utilization of the resource which can reasonably be expected to affect significantly the environment in the territory of the other State or States; and (b) upon request of the other State or States, to enter into consultations concerning the above mentioned plans; and (c) to provide, upon request to that effect to the other State or States, specific additional pertinent information concerning such plans, and (d) if there has been no advance notification as envisaged in sub-paragraph (a) above, to enter into consultations about such plans upon request of the other State or States.[49]

The Guidelines and Principles received a major endorsement from the United Nations General Assembly (UNGA) soon after they were adopted. The UNGA requested all States

> to use the Principles as guidelines and recommendations in the formulation of bilateral or multilateral conventions regarding natural resources shared by two or more States, on the basis of the principle of good faith and in the spirit of good neighborliness, and in such a way as to enhance and not to affect adversely development and the interests of all countries and in particular of the developing countries.[50]

The 1992 Rio Declaration on Environment and Development is another leading example on notification.[51] Principle 19 of the Rio Declaration, in line with the UNEP Guidelines and Principles, reads:

---

49 The UNEP Guidelines and Principles are available at: https://dirittointernazionaledellambiente.files.wordpress.com/2010/03/1978-unep-principles-shared-resources.pdf. In addition, sub-paragraph 2 of Principle 6 states that, "[i]n cases where the transmission of certain information is prevented by national legislation or international conventions, the State or States withholding such information shall nevertheless, on the basis, in particular, of the principle of good faith and in the spirit of good neighborliness, cooperate with the other interested State or States with the aim of finding a satisfactory solution."

50 United Nations General Assembly, 'Co-operation in the field of the environment concerning natural resources shared by two or more states,' Resolution 34/186 (18 December 1979).

51 United Nations General Assembly, *Report of the United Nations Conference on Environment and Development*, UN Doc. A/CONF.151/26 (Vol. 1) (12 August 1992), Annex I: Rio Declaration on Environment and Development; 31 I.L.M. 874 (1992); also included as Annex 6, in S. M. A. Salman (ed.), *'Groundwater: Legal and Policy Perspectives'*, World Bank Technical Paper No. 456 (Washington, DC: World Bank, 1999), at 257.

> State shall provide prior and timely notification and relevant information to potentially affected States on activities that may have a significant adverse transboundary environmental effect and shall consult with those States at an early stage and in good faith.

The Rio Declaration, in essence, incorporated, summarized, and refined the normative content of notification included in earlier instruments.[52]

In addition to the resolutions and statements of the IIL and the ILA and the soft law instruments discussed above, a number of regional and bilateral treaties require notification of other riparians of planned measures on shared watercourses. One such regional treaty is the 1968 African Convention on the Conservation of Nature and Natural Resources. The Convention requires that "[w]here surface and underground water resources are shared by two or more of the contracting States, the latter shall act in consultation, and if the need arise, set up inter-State Commissions to study and resolve problems arising from the joint use of these resources, and for the joint development and conservation thereof."[53] Thus, the Convention incorporates not only the principle of consultation, but also, impliedly, the principles of notification and negotiations in good faith.

The 1973 Treaty between Uruguay and Argentina Concerning the Rio de la Plata and the corresponding Maritime Boundary includes detailed provisions on notification.[54] Such provisions include description of the works, the time frame for response, type of response, the right of the notified party to inspect the works, and dispute resolution in case of differences. These provisions are

52 In addition to Principle 19 of the Rio Declaration, *id.*, Principle 18 requires: "States shall immediately notify other states of any natural disasters or other emergencies that are likely to produce sudden harmful effects on the environment of those States. Every effort shall be made by the international community to help States so affected." For a detailed analysis of Principle 19 and the arguments that it reflects customary international law, *see* Boisson de Chazournes & Sangbana, *'Principle 19'*, *supra* note 1.

53 African Convention on the Conservation of Nature and Natural Resources, Algiers, 15 September 1968, art. V(2), in United Nations Food and Agriculture Organization (FAO), *Treaties Concerning the Non-Navigational Uses of International Watercourses: Africa*, FAO Legislative Study 61 (Rome: FAO, 1997), at 10.

54 Article 17 of the 1973 Treaty states: "If one party plans to build new channels, substantially modify or alter existing ones or carry out other works, it shall notify the Administrative Commission which shall determine on a preliminary basis and within a maximum period of 30 days whether the plan might cause significant damage to the navigation interests of the other party or the regime of the river." Treaty Concerning the Río de la Plata and the Corresponding Maritime Boundary, Montevideo, 19 November 1973, 1295 U.N.T.S. 293 (1982). For discussion of the Treaty, *see* L. del Castillo-Laborde, *The Río de la Plata and its Maritime Front Legal Regime* (Leiden/Boston: Martinus Nijhoff Publishers, 2008).

reiterated and elaborated in the 1975 Statute of the River Uruguay concluded between Argentina and Uruguay, referred to in the discussion of the *Pulp Mills* case above.[55] Article 7 of the 1975 Statute specifically states that:

> If one party plans to construct new channels, substantially modify or alter existing ones or carry out any other works which are liable to affect navigation, the régime of the river or the quality of its waters, it shall notify the Commission, which shall determine on a preliminary basis and within a maximum period of 30 days whether the plan might cause significant damage to the other party.
>
> If the Commission finds this to be the case, or if a decision cannot be reached in that regard, the party concerned shall notify the other party of the plan through the said Commission.
>
> Such notification shall describe the main aspects of the work and, where appropriate, how it is to be carried out and shall include any other technical data that will enable the notified party to assess the probable impact of such works on navigation, the régime of the river or the quality of its waters.

It should be added that this is the article that the ICJ had the opportunity to comment on and to endorse, both on its procedural and substantive normative contents, as discussed above.

The 1991 United Nations Economic Commission for Europe (UNECE) Convention on Environmental Impact Assessment in a Transboundary Context (the Espoo Convention) requires notification by the Party of origin[56] for any proposed activity listed in Appendix I to the Convention that is likely to cause another party significant adverse transboundary impact. The list

55 Statute of the River Uruguay, *supra* note 7.

56 Convention on Environmental Impact Assessment in a Transboundary Context (Espoo Convention), 25 February 1991, entered in to force 25 September 1997; 1989 U.N.T.S. 310 (1997); 30 I.L.M. 800 (1991). Article 3 of the Espoo Convention states:

1. For a proposed activity listed in Appendix I that is likely to cause a significant adverse transboundary impact, the Party of origin shall, for the purposes of ensuring adequate and effective consultations under Article 5, notify any Party which it considers may be an affected Party as early as possible and no later than when informing its own public about that proposed activity.

This notification shall contain, *inter alia*: (a) Information on the proposed activity, including any available information on its possible transboundary impact; (b) The nature of the possible decision; and (c) An indication of a reasonable time within which a response under paragraph 3 of this Article is required, taking into account the nature of the proposed activity; and may include the information set out in paragraph 5 of this Article.

of such impacts includes waste water disposal, large dams and reservoirs, as well as groundwater abstraction.[57] Similarly, the 1992 UNECE Convention on the Protection and Use of Transboundary Watercourses and International Lakes (the Helsinki Convention) requires the parties to provide for the widest exchange of information, as early as possible, on issues covered under its provisions.[58] Article 10 of the Helsinki Convention calls for consultations, to be conducted on the basis of reciprocity, good faith, and good neighbourliness.

Some recent treaties have gone a step further and defined the term 'notification.' The Mekong Agreement 1995, for example, defines notification as "the timely providing of information by a riparian to the Joint Committee on its proposed use of water according to the format, content and procedures set forth in the Rules for Water Utilization and Inter-Basin Diversions under Article 26."[59] Thus, when the International Law Commission (ILC) started working on the Watercourses Convention in 1971, and by the time it had completed its work in 1994, and got the Convention adopted by the UNGA in 1997, a vast body of legal literature existed, or was emerging, in the field of international water law generally, and on notification specifically. Such literature reflected established and emerging principles and provided the basis of the work of the ILC in the field of notification, as will be discussed in the next part of this monograph.

---

57 *Id.*, Appendix I (List of Activities), para. 12.

58 Convention on the Protection and Use of Transboundary Watercourses and International Lakes (Helsinki Convention), Helsinki, 17 March 1992, entered into force 6 October 1996; 1936 U.N.T.S. 269 (2001); 31 I.L.M. 1312 (1992). In 2003, seven years after entry into force, the Convention was amended to allow accession by non-ECE countries. The amendment entered into force on 6 February 2013, ten years later, allowing the regional Helsinki Convention to become a global treaty to which all UN member states can accede. As of April 2019, Chad and Senegal are the only two non-ECE countries that have become members of the Convention. Indeed, Chad is the only country outside the ECE region that is a member of both Conventions; Senegal is not yet a party to the UN Watercourses Convention. *See* Salman, *Entry into Force of the UN Watercourses Convention*, *supra* note 2. As of April 2019, the Convention has 43 parties; *see* https://treaties.un.org/Pages/ViewDetails.aspx?src=TREATY&mtdsg_no=XXVII-5&chapter=27&clang=_en. Thus, there are two global treaties on shared watercourses in force; an unusual situation in the field of international law.

59 Agreement on the Cooperation for the Sustainable Development of the Mekong River Basin (Mekong Agreement), 5 April 1995, 34 I.L.M. 864 (1995), c. II (Definition of Terms). Article 26 of the Agreement requires the Joint Committee to prepare and propose for approval of the Council, *inter alia*, Rules for Water Utilization and Inter-Basin Diversions. Those Rules have been prepared and were approved by the Council in 2003 and include "Procedures for Notification, Prior Consultation and Agreement." *See* http://www.mrcmekong.org/download/programmes/PNPCA.pdf. For a detailed discussion of the Rules, *see* A. Rieu-Clarke, *'Notification and Consultation Procedures under the Mekong Agreement: Insights from the Xayaburi Controversy'*, 5:1 Asian Journal of International Law (2015) 143–175.

Part 3: The UN Watercourses Convention Provisions on Notification

Codification of international water law began only in 1970. On 8 December of that year, the UNGA adopted Resolution 2669 (XXV) asking its legal arm, the ILC,[60] to start working on a draft convention on the law of the non-navigational uses of international watercourses. The ILC started its work on the draft convention at its twenty-third session in December 1971. After close to a quarter of a century, five rapporteurs, and fifteen reports, the ILC completed its work, adopted the draft United Nations Convention on the Law of the Non-Navigational Uses of International Watercourses, and recommended it to the UNGA in June 1994.[61] It took three more years of deliberations by the UNGA's legal drafting committee, the "Sixth Committee," acting as a Working Group of the Whole, in two contentious sessions, before the UNGA itself finally adopted the Watercourses Convention and opened it for signature on 21 May 1997.[62] It was only on 17 August 2014 that the Convention entered into force and effect, more than seventeen years after its adoption by the UNGA, and close to 45 years after the adoption of Resolution 2669.[63]

The Preamble to the Watercourses Convention recalled "the existing bilateral and multilateral agreements regarding the non-navigational uses of international watercourses."[64] The Preamble also acknowledged "the valuable contribution of international organizations, both governmental and non-governmental, to the codification and progressive development of

60 The ILC is a UN body composed of legal experts, nominated by states and elected by the UNGA, and tasked with the codification and progressive development of international law.

61 *See* R. Rosenstock, '*Second Report on the Law of the Non-navigational Uses of International Watercourses by Mr. Robert Rovenstock, Special Rapporteur*', II (2) Yearbook of International Law Commission (1994) 88–135, at 88.

62 The Convention is annexed to UNGA Resolution 51/229, 21 May 1997; *see also* 36 ILM 700 (1997). The Convention was adopted by a vote of 103 for and three against (Burundi, China and Turkey), with 27 abstentions. *See also* Salman, *Entry into Force of the UN Watercourses Convention, supra* note 2.

63 As of March 2019, the Watercourses Convention has 36 parties; *see* https://treaties.un.org/Pages/ViewDetails.aspx?src=IND&mtdsg_no=XXVII-12&chapter=27&clang=_en.

64 It should be stated that two conventions related to the uses of international watercourses were in force at that time: (i) the 1921 Convention and Statute on the Regime of Navigable Waterways of International Concern, which is also known as the Barcelona Convention, and (ii) the 1923 General Convention Relating to the Development of Hydraulic Power Affecting More Than One State, which is also known as the Geneva Convention. However, both conventions dealt with specific limited issues and did not lay down generally applicable principles regulating the use and protection of international watercourses. Moreover, few countries were parties at that time (and indeed now) to either of these conventions.

international law in this field." Thus, the ILC made explicit references to, and acknowledged the contribution of regional treaties, judicial decisions, and soft law instruments to the evolution and progressive development of international water law.[65]

It should be noted at the outset that the different rapporteurs of the ILC were in agreement that the duty to notify other states of planned measures on the shared watercourse is "an expression of a prevailing principle of international law."[66] Thus, the time and energy of the different ILC rapporteurs were spent in working out the details of the notification requirement, rather than in debating the concept itself, as happened with other principles of international water law.

The Watercourses Convention is divided into seven parts and one annex on arbitration. Part III of the Convention deals with notification and includes nine articles (11 to 19) thereon.[67]

Article 11 of the Watercourses Convention lays the roadmap for notification, starting with the effects of planned measures on the shared watercourse itself, before addressing the effects on the other riparians. The Article requires watercourse states to exchange information and consult each other and, if necessary, negotiate over the possible effects of planned measures on the condition of an international watercourse.

Article 12 lays down the general rule regarding notification. The Article requires notification of the other watercourse states before the state implements or permits implementation of planned measures that may have significant adverse effect upon other watercourse states.

It should be noted that the Watercourses Convention has used throughout its provisions, the term 'watercourse state' and not the terms 'downstream' and 'upstream' riparians. Article 12 has also established the threshold of 'significant adverse effect' that may result from the planned measures as the trigger for notification. Article 12 of the Convention goes on to require notification of other watercourse states. The term 'other watercourse states' should be understood to include all other riparians, whether downstream or upstream.

---

65 For an analysis of the relationship between these levels of regulation, *see* L. Boisson de Chazournes, *Freshwater and International Law, supra* note 37.

66 *See* S. Schwebel, *'Third Report on the Law of the Non-navigational Uses of International Watercourses'*, II (1) Yearbook of the International Law Commission (1982), UN Doc. A/CN.4/348 and Corr. 1, 65–191.

67 For a detailed discussion of these articles *see* K. Sangbana, *'Notification and Consultation Concerning Planned Measures'*, in Boisson de Chazournes et al (eds.) *The UN Convention, supra* note 18.

As mentioned above, one of the major misunderstandings about international water law is that harm can only be caused by upstream riparians to those downstream of the shared watercourse. Based on this faulty belief, it is widely thought by a large segment of water resources specialists, both lawyers and non-lawyers, that notification is the duty of upstream riparians only, and is the exclusive right of downstream riparians, because only upstream riparians can harm downstream riparians.

It is obvious, and clearer, that downstream riparians can be harmed by the physical impacts of water quantity and quality changes caused by use of the watercourse by the upstream riparians. The quantity of water flow can be decreased by the upstream riparians through construction of dams, canals and pipelines, and through the storage and diversion of the waters of the shared rivers. The quality of the water of the shared rivers can be affected by the upstream riparians through pollution caused by industrial waste, sewage, or agricultural run-off.

It is much less obvious, and generally not realized, that the upstream riparians can be affected, or even harmed, by the potential foreclosure of their future use of water caused by the prior use and the claiming of rights to such water by the downstream riparians. Projects on shared rivers in the downstream riparian states would help those riparians in acquiring, and later claiming, rights to the water abstracted under those projects. The availability and use of such waters in future by the upper riparians would have already been foreclosed by the downstream riparians.

Such downstream riparians would usually invoke the principle of acquired rights and the obligation not to cause harm in the face of claims by the upstream riparians. The upstream riparians' claims to part of the waters of the shared watercourse under the principle of equitable and reasonable utilization would be countered by claims of historic rights and existing uses, and the obligation against causing harm by affecting such rights and uses.[68]

As an example of how downstream riparians can harm upstream ones, a poor upstream country could be precluded from developing the water resources of a shared river in the near future if a richer downstream riparian, without consultation or notification, develops it at present. The downstream state would establish rights to those waters, which they would claim as acquired rights, thus foreclosing the future uses of those waters by the upstream

68 *See* Salman, *'The Obligation'*, *supra* note 18; *see also* Salman, *'Downstream Riparians'*, *supra* note 18.

riparians.[69] Thus, just as upstream riparians can harm downstream ones through storage, diversion, and use of the waters of the shared rivers, downstream riparians can also harm upstream riparians by foreclosing their future uses of the shared waters through the prior use of, and the claiming of rights to such water, and invoking the no harm obligation.

The World Bank policies for Projects on International Waterways, as will be discussed in the next two parts of this monograph, have amply clarified the concept of foreclosure of future uses through the strict requirement that all riparians, whether downstream or upstream, should be notified of all projects on the shared waterway. Indeed, some countries have understood this and are aware of this concept of international water law,[70] and some recent treaties have incorporated the concept.[71]

---

69 *See* S. McCaffrey, *'Water Disputes Defined: Characteristics and Trends for Resolving Them'*, in The Permanent Court of Arbitration (ed.), *Resolution of International Water Disputes* (Kluwer Law International, 2003) 49–90, at 59; *see also* Salman, *supra* note 18.

70 One example of the comprehension of the concept of foreclosure of future uses is the note sent by the then Prime Minister of India, Mr. Jawaharlal Nehru, to the then President of Pakistan, Mr. Mohammad Ayub Khan in 1961, on their dispute over the Ganges River which India and Pakistan shared at that time, before the birth of Bangladesh in 1971. In that note Mr. Nehru wrote: "One more matter to which I must also refer, is the distinction you still seem to make between the rights of upper and lower riparians in paragraph 7 of your letter, which implies that the lower riparian can proceed unilaterally with projects, while the upper riparian should not be free to do so. If this was to be so, it would enable the lower riparian to create, unilaterally, historic rights in its favor and go on inflating them at its discretion thereby completely blocking all development and uses of the upper riparian. We cannot, obviously, accept this point of view." *See* B. Crow, *Sharing the Ganges: The Politics and Technology of River Development* (New Delhi: Sage Publications, 1995), at 89. Another example is Ethiopia's Note Verbale of 20 March 1997, addressed to Egypt and copied to the Mr. Kofi Annan, Secretary-General of the United Nations, Mr. Salim Ahmed Salim, Secretary-General of the Organization of the African Unity (OAU), and Mr. James Wolfensohn, President of the World Bank. The Note, as quoted by John Waterbury, stated: "Ethiopia wishes to be on record as having made it unambiguously clear that it will not allow its share to the Nile waters to be affected by a *fait accompli* such as the Toshka project, regarding which it was neither consulted nor alerted." *See* J. Waterbury, *The Nile Basin* (Yale University Press, 2002) at 84–5. The Toshka Project involved the irrigation of about 200,000 hectares in the southwestern desert of Egypt through a pumping station and canal that would convey water from the Aswan High Dam.

71 The Senegal River Water Charter was concluded by Senegal, Mauritania, and Mali in May 2002 and signed by Guinea in 2006. Article 4 enumerates a number of principles for distribution of the water of the Senegal River, including "the obligation of each riparian state before engaging in any activity or project likely to have an impact on water availability and/or the possibility to implement future projects." For more information on the Senegal River agreements, *see* B. A. Godana, *Africa's Shared Water Resources, Legal and Institutional Aspects of the Nile, Niger and Senegal River Systems* (Francis Pinter Publishers, 1985); *see*

It should be noted that Article 12 of the Watercourses Convention has used the threshold of 'significant adverse effect'[72] resulting from the planned measure on the shared watercourses for the notification to become a requirement. Realizing that this term may have different interpretations by different riparians, the Sixth Committee, convening as the Working Group of the Whole, attempted to clarify what the term means. In a Statement of Understanding,[73] the Working Group stated:

> The term "significant" is not used in this article or elsewhere in the present Convention in the sense of "substantial." What is to be avoided are localized agreements, or agreements concerning a particular project, programme or use, which have a significant effect upon third Watercourse States. While such an effect must be capable of being established by objective evidence and not be trivial in nature, it need not rise to the level of being substantial.[74]

This Statement of Understanding seems to comport with and endorse that of the ILC which stated during the preparation of the draft Convention that 'significant adverse effect' refers to a level of severity less than that of the term 'significant harm.'[75]

Article 12 goes on to add substantive obligations to the procedural content of Article 11. The Article requires the notifying state to accompany the notification to the notified states with "available technical data and information, including the results of any environmental impact assessment, in order to enable the notified States to evaluate the possible effects of the planned measures."

---

also N. C. Odili, *'Shared Water Resources in West Africa: Relevance and Application of the UN Watercourses and the UNECE Water Conventions'*, 3:1 International Water Law (2018).

72 It should be noted that Article 7 of the Watercourses Convention, *supra* note 62, obliges the watercourse states not to cause 'significant harm', while the threshold for notification under Article 12 of the Convention is 'significant adverse effect.'

73 These Statements of Understanding, issued by the Sixth Committee convened as a Working Group of the Whole, covered various issues, including clarifications to some of the terms used in the draft Convention. For the Report of the Six Committee Convening as the Working Group of the Whole, UN Doc. A/51/869 (11 April 1997), available at: http://www.un.org/law/cod/watere.htm.

74 *Id.* In earlier drafts of the Convention the threshold used was 'appreciable adverse effects'; *see* United Nations, Report of the International Law Commission on the Work of its Fortieth Session, 9 May–29 July 1988 (Supplement No. 10, UN Doc. A/43/10, New York, 1988), at 79; *see also* Salman, *'The Obligation' supra* note 18.

75 Rosenstock, *supra* note 61, at 111, commentary (2) to Article 12.

One question that this language raises is whether the Convention obliges the states planning measures on the shared watercourse to undertake an environmental impact assessment (EIA) for such measures. A close reading of Article 12 would lead to the conclusion that the Article does not require undertaking an EIA; perhaps it is only suggestive of carrying out such an assessment. However, the ICJ decision in *Pulp Mills* mandated the carrying out of such an EIA.[76]

Article 13 deals with the period for reply by the notified state, and establishes six months as the period within which the notified state would study and evaluate the possible effects of the planned measures and would communicate the findings to the notifying state. Such period of six months can be extended, at the request of the notified state, for another period of six months.

One general comment on this article is that the proposed period, which can total one year at this stage, is a little bit long and can delay unnecessarily the carrying out of planned measures that would not cause any adverse effects. Perhaps the extension period could have been cut down to three months. As discussed below, the World Bank Procedures also specify a period not exceeding six months as the time for reply to the notification. However, the Bank has in practice established a shorter period, ranging in most cases between 30 and 60 days, subject to an extension of 30 days.[77]

Article 14 deals with the obligations of the notifying state during the period for reply. The Article obliges the notifying state to cooperate with the notified states by providing them, on request, with any additional data and information that is available and necessary for an accurate evaluation of the planned measure. However, Article 31 of the Watercourses Convention qualifies this obligation, and clarifies that "[n]othing in the present Convention obliges a watercourse State to provide data or information vital to its national defense or security. Nevertheless, that State shall cooperate in good faith with the other watercourse States with a view to providing as much information as possible under the circumstances."

76 The ICJ stated: "In this sense, the obligation to protect and preserve, under Article 41 (*a*) of the Statute, has to be interpreted in accordance with a practice, which in recent years has gained so much acceptance among States that it may now be considered a requirement under general international law to undertake an environmental impact assessment where there is a risk that the proposed industrial activity may have a significant adverse impact in a transboundary context, in particular, on a shared resource. Moreover, due diligence, and the duty of vigilance and prevention which it implies, would not be considered to have been exercised, if a party planning works liable to affect the régime of the river or the quality of its waters did not undertake an environmental impact assessment on the potential effects of such works." *Pulp Mills* case, *supra* note 6, para. 204.

77 This issue is discussed in detail in part 5.6 of this monograph.

Article 14 goes on to require the notified state not to implement or permit implementation of the planned measures without the consent of the notified States. However, this consent is only required for implementation of the planned measures during the period for reply. It is not a veto power over the planned measure as a whole. The various possible kinds of reply that may ensue from such notification, and the process to be followed if the notifying state receives an objection (or no-consent) by one or more of the notified states for carrying out the planned measures are discussed further below.

Article 15 deals with the reply to notification. The Article requires the notified states to communicate their findings to the notifying state as early as possible within the period applicable pursuant to Article 13. If a notified state finds that implementation of the planned measures would be inconsistent with the provisions of Articles 5 or 7 of the Convention, it shall attach to its finding a documented explanation setting forth the reasons for the finding. It should be added that Article 5 of the Convention deals with equitable and reasonable utilization and participation, while Article 7 deals with the obligation not to cause significant harm. Thus, Article 15 underscores the concept of foreclosure of future uses discussed above by requiring the planned measures to be consistent with the principle of equitable and reasonable utilizations which applies to all the watercourse states.[78]

Article 16 addresses the issue of the absence of reply to notification. The Article authorizes the notifying state, if it has received no communication under Article 15, subject to its obligations under Articles 5 and 7 referred to above, to proceed with implementation of the planned measures, in accordance with the notification and any other data and information provided to the notified States. Article 16 goes on to state that any claim to compensation by a notified state that has failed to reply within the period applicable pursuant to Article 13 may be offset by the costs incurred by the notifying state for action undertaken after the expiration of the time for a reply which would not have been undertaken if the notified state had objected within that period.

Article 17 deals with consultations and negotiations concerning the planned measures. It stipulates that if the notified state receives a communication that implementation of the planned measures would be inconsistent with the provisions of Articles 5 or 7 of the Convention, the notifying state and the state making the communication shall enter into consultations and, if necessary, negotiations with a view to arriving at an equitable resolution of the situation.[79] The Article goes on to require that the consultations and negotiations be

78 *See* Salman, *'The Obligation'*, *supra* note 18; Salman, *'Downstream Riparians'*, *supra* note 18.

79 *See* Farrajota, *supra* note 3.

conducted on the basis that each state must in good faith pay reasonable regard to the rights and legitimate interests of the other state.[80] Thus, the notified states have no veto power over the planned measure, as will be discussed in part 7 of this monograph. Further, Article 17 requires that during the course of the consultations and negotiations, the notifying state shall, if so requested by the notified state at the time it makes the communication, refrain from implementing or permitting the implementation of the planned measures for a period of six months, unless otherwise agreed. Thus, the period for processing the notification and its results can be as long as 18 months – which is quite a long period.

Procedures in the absence of notification are dealt with in Article 18 of the Convention. The Article authorizes a watercourse state that has reasonable grounds to believe that another watercourse state is planning measures that may have a significant adverse effect upon it, to request the latter to apply the provisions of Article 12. The request shall be accompanied by a documented explanation setting forth its grounds.[81] The Article goes on to address the situation where the state planning the measures finds that it is not under an obligation to provide a notification under Article 12. In such case, Article 18 authorizes the state planning the measures to inform the other state, and to provide a documented explanation setting forth the reasons for such finding. If this finding does not satisfy the other state, the two states shall, at the request of that other state, promptly enter into consultations and negotiations in the manner indicated in paragraphs 1 and 2 of Article 17. The Article goes on to stipulate that during the course of the consultations and negotiations, the state planning the measures shall, if so requested by the other state at the time it requests the initiation of consultations and negotiations, refrain from implementing or permitting the implementation of those measures for a period of six months unless otherwise agreed.

Article 19 addresses the issue of urgent implementation of planned measures. It states that in the event that implementation of planned measures is of the utmost urgency in order to protect public health, public safety or other equally important interests, the state planning the measures may, subject to Articles 5 and 7, immediately proceed to implementation, notwithstanding the provisions of Article 14, and paragraph 3 of Article 17. Article 19 goes on to require that in such case, a formal declaration of the urgency of the measures shall be communicated without delay to the other watercourse states, together

80 *See* Leb, *supra* note 4.

81 This is the third situation regarding notification identified and discussed by Professor Charles Bourne, *supra* note 5.

with the relevant data and information. However, the article requires the state planning the measures, at the request of any of the states notified of urgent implementation of planned measures, to promptly enter into consultations and negotiations with it in the manner indicated in Article 17.[82]

In addition to these nine articles, mention should be made of Article 30 in Part VI (Miscellaneous Provisions) of the Watercourses Convention on 'indirect procedures.' It states that in cases where there are serious obstacles to direct contacts between watercourse states, the states concerned shall fulfil their obligations of cooperation provided for in the present Convention, including exchange of data and information, notification, communication, consultations and negotiations, through any indirect procedure accepted by them. The Article is not included in Part III on notification because it deals with indirect procedures for a number of aspects concerning riparian relations, of which notification is only one. However, as will be discussed in the next part of this monograph, notification is indeed the most important challenge to riparians' relations when there are serious obstacles to direct contacts between the watercourse states concerned.

Furthermore, Article 28 of the Convention addresses the issue of notification in emergency situations. The Article stipulates that a watercourse state shall, without delay and by the most expeditious means available, notify other potentially affected states and competent international organizations of any emergency originating within its territory. However, since this article does not deal with planned measures, but rather with emergency situations,[83] it does not fall within the scope of this monograph, and as such is not included in the discussion and analysis of the provisions of the Convention dealing with notification for planned measures of this monograph.

Thus, the ten articles of the UN Watercourses Convention discussed above have laid down detailed procedures for notification concerning planned measures on shared watercourses, as well as for the reply to notification and for processes for resolving any differences arising therefrom. Indeed, these articles, in addition to Article 28 referred to above, encompass the three types of

82 For a thorough analysis of these articles on notification, *see* S. McCaffrey, *The Law of International Watercourses* (2nd ed., Oxford: Oxford University Press, 2007); A. Tanzi & M. Arcari, *The United Nations Convention on the Law of International Watercourses* (The Hague: Kluwer, 2001); Farrajota, *supra* note 3; Leb, *supra* note 4; Salman, *'Entry into Force'*, *supra* note 2.

83 Article 28 of the Convention defines 'emergency' to mean "a situation that causes, or poses an imminent threat of causing, serious harm to watercourse States or other States and that results suddenly from natural causes, such as floods, the breaking up of ice, landslides or earthquakes, or from human conduct, such as industrial accidents."

notification enumerated by Professor Charles Bourne and discussed above.[84] However, the practical and implementation experience of the World Bank with regards to notification as set forth in the provisions of the Bank Policy for Projects on International Waterways shows more complex and challenging contours and details for this process, as will be discussed in the next two parts of this monograph.

Part 4: The World Bank Early Approaches and Policies on Notification

4.1 *Facing the Challenges of Projects on Shared Watercourses*

The World Bank faced the issue of how to deal with projects on international waterways soon after it commenced operational work in 1946.[85] The Bank noted immediately that a number of hydropower, irrigation, water supply and industrial projects that it started financing were on shared watercourses and were thus likely to have an imopact on the quantity or quality of the shared waters and on the interests of other riparian states. Those types of projects, it was soon realized, could affect the relations between the Bank and its borrowers, as well as between the riparian states themselves. Accordingly, the Bank, with its special status as an international cooperative financial institution (owned, with varying shares, by the very same members it serves), had to decide how to handle this delicate triangular relationship and the circumstances surrounding such projects.[86]

However, international water law at that time – in the late 1940s and early 1950s – was in the infancy stage. There were no established rules regulating

84 *Supra* note 5.

85 The Articles of Agreement of the International Bank for Reconstruction and Development (IBRD, or the Bank) were discussed and agreed upon during a meeting that was held in Bretton Woods, New Hampshire, in July 1944, and entered into force on 27 December 1945. The Bank opened for business on 25 June 1946, two years after the Bretton Woods meeting, with the Bank membership reaching 38 states at the time of the meeting. The Articles of Agreement are available at: http://web.worldbank.org/WBSITE/EXTERNAL/EXTABOUTUS/0,,contentMDK:20049557~pagePK:51123644~piPK:329829~theSitePK:29708,00.html. *See also* E. S. Mason & R. E. Asher, *The World Bank since Bretton Woods* (Washington, DC: The Brookings Institution, 1973).

86 For a detailed historical account and analysis of the World Bank policies for projects on international waterways, *see* S. M. A. Salman, *The World Bank Policy for Projects on International Waterways: An Historical and Legal Analysis* (Leiden: Martinus Nijhoff Publishers, 2009; Washington, DC: World Bank, 2009). This part of the monograph, as well as the next part, are based on, and draw largely from, documents and information contained in this book.

the uses and protection of shared watercourses.[87] A few tribunal decisions laid down some general international law principles, the application of which could be extended to shared watercourses. One such decision is the *Trail Smelter* case, which established responsibility of the state for using its territory in such a manner as not to cause harm to other states.[88] The *Lake Lanoux Arbitration* tribunal, discussed above, ruled that although France was entitled to use the waters of Lake Lanoux, which it shares with Spain, it could not ignore Spain's interests.[89] As such, there were no universally established or agreed upon principles that the Bank could rely on. The Bank had to develop its approaches and policies for dealing with the riparian issues related to projects on shared watercourses it planned to finance without the benefit of established, or even emerging, principles of international water law. As will be discussed in this part of the monograph, these two cases have, nevertheless, influenced the World Bank policies for Projects on International Waterways considerably.

Additionally, international water disputes started cropping up, particularly with the increase in the number of states gaining independence from their colonial powers. The Indus and the Nile River disputes were examples of the difficulties that the World Bank, as an international cooperative financial institution, faced, and which had major effects on the Bank lending program for projects involving these basins. As the then President of the World Bank, Eugene Black, noted on the Indus dispute:

> Not only did the Indus issue stand in the way of constructive action by the Bank in the subcontinent, it was a cause for concern in a wider sense. With two of the Bank's potentially largest customers so bitterly opposed, the world's investors might regard the Bank's own prospects with a skepticism that would cripple its ability to raise money through borrowing.[90]

87 As noted above (*supra* note 64), the 1921 Barcelona Convention and the 1923 Geneva Convention were in force at that time.

88 In 1941, the arbitration tribunal in the *Trail Smelter* case concluded that "no state has the right to use or permit the use of its territory in such a manner as to cause injury by fumes in or to the territory of another or the properties or persons therein, when the case is of serious consequence and the injury is established by clear and convincing evidence." *See Trail Smelter Arbitration* (*United States v. Canada*), 3 R.I.A.A. 1911 (1941), at 1965. The application of this principle was extended to international watercourses, basically strengthening the obligation against causing harm.

89 *See Lake Lanoux Arbitration, supra* note 30.

90 Mason & Asher, *supra* note 85, at 612, quoting Eugene R. Black, *'The Indus: A Moral for Nations'*, *The New York Times* (11 December 1960).

Thus, the lack of globally agreed upon principles on international water law, and the existing and emerging disputes on shared watercourses prompted, indeed pushed, the Bank to search and adopt approaches and policies for its increasing number of projects on shared watercourses.

The Bank's initial approach towards projects on international waterways developed on a somewhat *ad hoc* basis. The Bank, for example, did not finance any projects on any river where there was a dispute, and insisted that an agreement be reached first. However, the Bank soon realized that agreements on shared watercourses are not easy to conclude, and would take years to negotiate, as evidenced by its own experience with the Indus Basin dispute, where the negotiations took ten years before the Indus Waters Treaty was concluded in 1960.[91] At the same time, the pressure and need to adopt clearer approaches and policies was growing.

Indeed, the need for new approaches and policies was dictated by a number of factors which still apply today. Now and then, before any loan is made by the Bank, the merits of the proposed project must be carefully studied.[92] Moreover, the Bank, as an international cooperative financial institution, owes certain duties to all its members (the borrower as well as the other riparians in such projects), and is required by its Articles of Agreement to "act prudently in the interests both of the particular member in whose territories the project is located and of the members as a whole."[93] Thus, in considering a loan for a project involving the use of the waters of an international waterway, the Bank has to, and should ensure that the proposed uses will not be harmful to the interests of other riparians, whether upstream or downstream. It should also ensure that the proposed project will not be adversely affected by other riparians' uses of the international waterway. Additionally, the Bank should also ensure that the project is not inconsistent with international law, or with the provisions of any bilateral or multilateral treaty to which the beneficiary state is a party, and that there is no dispute on the shared watercourse in question.[94]

---

91 *See* Salman & Uprety, *Conflict and Cooperation*, *supra* note 32.

92 Article III, Section 4 (iii) of the Articles of Agreement of the Bank, *supra* note 85, specifies, as one of the conditions for making a loan or a guarantee, that "a competent committee ... has submitted a written report recommending the project after a careful study of the proposal."

93 *Id.*, art. III, Section 4 (v).

94 For further discussion of these approaches and issues, *see* R. Krishna, *'Evolution and Context of the Bank Policy for Projects on International Waterways'*, in S. M. A. Salman & L. Boisson de Chazournes (eds.), *International Watercourses: Enhancing Cooperation and Managing Conflict*, World Bank Technical Paper No. 414 (Washington, DC: The World Bank, 1998), at 31.

4.2 *Searching for an Approach*

A number of proposed projects in the 1950s, including the Youssef Pasha and the Ghab Projects in Syria, the Aswan High Dam Project in Egypt, the Bhakra-Nagal Dam Project in India, and the Lower Sind Barrage Project in Pakistan all involved international rivers.[95] At that time, however, none of those rivers – the Orontes, Euphrates, Nile, or the Indus – had an agreement governing the uses and sharing of its waters. Moreover, actual disputes between some of the riparians of those rivers had already emerged and disputes with other riparians were expected to arise as a result of the proposed projects.

Consequently, one early approach of the Bank to projects on international rivers was to distinguish between rivers over which there were disputes, and those over which no apparent disputes existed at the time the project was being considered for financing. This approach was applied as early as 1949–1950 when the Bank was considering financing the Bakhra-Nangal Project in India and the Lower Sind Barrage Project in Pakistan. Both projects were on the Indus River System, over which a dispute had already erupted in 1948 following the partitioning of the sub-continent. Because of the dispute, and the objection of both India and Pakistan to the Bank financing of projects on the disputed Indus River System in the territory of the other country, the Bank was not able to extend funding to either project.[96]

Similarly, the circumstances that surrounded the efforts to negotiate financing for the Aswan High Dam Project in Egypt in the early to mid-1950s were quite complex. The dispute over the sharing of the waters of the Nile River between Egypt and Sudan at that time was only one of many issues that dominated the discussion between the Bank and Egypt.[97] The Bank reached a determination from the start that financing the Aswan High Dam scheme would depend on Egypt's concluding an agreement with the Sudan, and perhaps other upstream countries, about sharing the waters of the Nile.

Accordingly, the Bank had to balance the competing demands and interests of the different riparians over the limited amount of waters of the shared watercourse on the one hand, and its character and responsibilities, as an

---

95 For more discussion on these projects *see id.*

96 Mason & Asher, *supra* note 85, at 612. *See* also Undala Z. Alam, *'Water Rationality: Mediating the Indus Waters Treaty'* (Unpublished Ph.D. thesis, University of Durham, United Kingdom, 1998) at 97. It is worth adding that the failure of the Bank to finance either of these projects was one reason for the Bank to offer its good offices to India and Pakistan in an attempt to find a solution to the dispute, *see* Salman & Uprety, *Shared Watercourses*, *supra* note 10.

97 For discussion of the Aswan High Dam Project and the Bank involvement, *see* Mason & Asher, *supra* note 85, at 627–643.

international cooperative financial institution, on the other. This task has proven throughout the years to be quite intricate and complex, requiring a very delicate and careful handling.

These difficulties showed themselves amply in other cases, including two projects the Bank was studying at that time in Syria: the Youssef Pasha Dam Project on the Orontes River,[98] and the Ghab Project on the Euphrates River.[99] There were no actual disputes at that time on the Orontes or the Euphrates Rivers. However, given the absence of an agreement on both rivers, the history of the relationship between the riparian states of those rivers, and the nature of the projects which involved, *inter alia*, construction of dams, there were concerns that the projects might generate protests from the other riparians. There was also concern that those projects could also ignite disputes among the riparian states, as well as with the Bank itself. Dispute avoidance with and among riparians as a result of a Bank-financed project was, and continues to be, a major objective for the Bank. Although those two projects presented major challenges to the Bank, they also provided the Bank with an opportunity to deliberate on possible generic approaches for its funded projects on shared rivers.

The Youssef Pasha Project involved the construction of a multipurpose dam on the Euphrates River for regulation of the river flow, irrigation during the dry season, and generation of hydroelectric power. The Bank took note of the international character of the Euphrates River, and the stalled discussions of the riparians on how to share it. It concluded that there was a need for some form of international cooperation between the three riparian countries (Turkey, Syria and Iraq), before financing of the project could be considered. Various possible approaches were contemplated within the Bank. One approach was the conclusion of an agreement by the three riparians to establish a Euphrates Commission whose function would be to study the overall problems affecting water control and the best utilization of the waters of the Euphrates River. A similar commission, it was thought, might function in connection with the utilization of the Tigris River.

---

98 The Orontes River rises in Lebanon, flows north through Syria for most of its course, forms the border between Syria and Turkey for approximately 25 miles, and then swings west and southwest through Turkey before it empties into the Mediterranean Sea. *See* G. Shapland, *Rivers of Discourse, International Water Disputes in the Middle East* (London: Hurst & Company, 1997).

99 The Euphrates River is shared by Turkey, Syria and Iraq. *See* J. Kolars, *'Problems of International River Management: The Case of the Euphrates'*, in A. K. Biswas (ed.), *International Waters of the Middle East: From Euphrates-Tigris to Nile* (Oxford: Oxford University Press, 1994), at 44.

When the Bank realized that the political situation was not conducive to the establishment of such a commission, other approaches were considered. One such approach was for Syria to discuss the proposed project with the Government of Iraq and, if necessary, reach some understanding on the minimum flow to be available in the Euphrates River for Iraq after the completion of the project. Similarly, the Bank concluded that this approach was not politically feasible. While the processing of the project continued, the issue of how to deal with the other riparians of the Euphrates River was overtaken in 1953 by the overall discussion and deliberations on similar issues related to the Ghab Project.

The Ghab Project involved the reclamation and development of the Ghab Valley in northwest Syria, through which the Orontes River flows.[100] The Project consisted of the drainage of extensive swamp lands and their upstream protection by a retention dam and other flood control and irrigation works, which included a storage dam and a system of distribution canals. The international aspects of the Orontes River and the Ghab Project triggered extensive discussion within the Bank, and set in motion a search for a general approach towards projects on international waters. The Bank was keenly aware of its peculiar responsibilities as an international cooperative financial institution. Accordingly, it was alert to the need for extreme care in extending a loan to one country, for a project that might adversely affect the physical conditions in another country, without the consent of the latter, expressed in a form satisfactory to the Bank.

During the deliberations on these two projects a number of possible generic approaches, applicable to other projects were raised and discussed.[101] One of those approaches was for the Bank to assist in regional planning through the establishment of an authority to study and determine the most effective ways of utilizing the waters of the shared river among the riparian countries, and to supervise the approved uses of such a river. However, the Bank realized, judging from the Indus and Nile negotiations underway at the time, that an agreement would take quite a while to reach, if indeed such an agreement was ever to materialize.

Another approach considered was for the Bank to require the consent of all the riparian states for the proposed project, following notification and provision of all information about the project. Concerns were raised, however, that

100 *See* Shapland, *supra* note 98.

101 For a more detailed discussion of those options, *see* R. Krishna, *International Waters in Bank Projects: History and Case Studies*, Legal Department Working Paper No. 2 (Washington, DC: World Bank 1973), at 14–25.

some riparians, with no real interest in the project, could cause delays, or even block the project, by failing to assent, or could use the request for assent to insist on quite unrelated concessions. The notion of giving veto power to one or more of the riparians was soon discarded based on the criticism of this approach, which was set out by the IIL in 1911 in the Madrid Declaration.

One generic alternative discussed was that the facts and circumstances of each case would determine how the Bank would discharge its duty in such projects. In other words, the Bank would follow an *ad hoc* approach. This flexible approach was based on the Bank ascertaining all pertinent facts related to the project, to the best of its ability, prior to making a final determination. The approach would include requiring the prospective borrower to satisfy the Bank that the project would not result in a substantive protest from another riparian whose interests might be affected by the project. It could be that the project would have no effects whatsoever on any other riparian. Conversely, it could have effects on the other riparians, and the Bank would have to seek a no-objection agreement from those countries. In this connection the Bank would have to keep in mind frivolous or unfounded objections, or objections used for bargaining purposes.[102]

Following this approach, the other riparians should be given a reasonable opportunity to consider the effects of the project on their interests and to express an opinion. This meant that the other riparians would be notified of the project and the project details, and be given an opportunity to convey their comments and views. However, the opinion of the other riparians would not prevent the Bank from making its own decision and determination on the project, taking into account all the pertinent facts. This meant that the consent of the other riparians was not essential, and that the Bank could still finance the project notwithstanding an objection from one or more of the riparians.

During these deliberations it was constantly repeated that the objection of another riparian country could be frivolous, or based only on a remote likelihood that this country would require the water itself within a reasonable period. It was also argued that the objection could be designed as leverage against the other country in some unrelated matter, or intended to gain some undue advantage in the immediate issue.

Although the deliberations raised several possible approaches, consensus seemed to be emerging by 1956 that the facts and circumstances of each case must determine how the Bank would handle the proposed project. This approach was referred to as the 'flexible approach',[103] and was reflected in the

102 *Id.*

103 Krishna, *'The Evolution and Context of the Bank Policy'*, *supra* note 94.

Bank policies for projects on international waterways that were subsequently adopted.

With regards to the Ghab Project, the Bank decided that the mere absence of an agreement between Turkey and Syria on the Orontes River or the project, should not prevent the Bank from participation in the financing of the project. Further, there was no real risk that possible uses of the water for irrigation before the river enters Syria would endanger the project. The Bank concluded that the Project would control winter floods of the Orontes and thus, in this respect, benefit the entire valley to the north. Finally, the Bank determined that there would continue to be sufficient summer flow of the water of the Orontes River below the Ghab to provide adequate water for all land presently irrigated and for all irrigable land not presently irrigated in the valley of the Orontes River between the Ghab and the mouth of the river.

A copy of the Project report was transmitted to Turkey in August 1955. Negotiations for the Project were completed in early 1956, but soon afterward, and before the Project was considered by the Executive Directors, the Bank was informed of Turkey's intention to object to the Project. Meanwhile, and as a result of the deliberations and developments on the processing of the Ghab Project, including the informal objection by Turkey, the Bank issued its first policy for projects on international waterways in March 1956, as discussed below. In May of that year, Turkey officially objected to the Ghab Project claiming that the Project would deprive it of the waters of the Orontes River during the irrigation season, and asked that the Project design be revised by experts from both governments. This objection was a significant milestone on the Bank's projects on international rivers, and was indeed a major factor in shaping its rethinking of the ways and means for dealing with such projects.

As a result of Turkey's objection and demand that the Project design be revised by Syrian and Turkish experts, the Syrian government informed the Bank of its decision to postpone consideration of the Ghab Project.[104] Thus, the processing of the Ghab Project ended before Board consideration. Nonetheless,

---

104 No reasons for the Syrian request for the postponement of the processing of the Project were included in any of the Bank records. In fact, processing of the Project stopped at that stage and was never revived. Greg Shapland gave the following explanation: "In response to Turkish claims to the region, the Hatay province into which the Orontes flows, was detached from Syria in the late 1930s when Syria was under the French mandate – essentially as a sop to Turkey to prevent it from siding with Nazi Germany. Although the Syrians must be well aware that there is no prospect of getting the region back in the foreseeable future, they maintain officially that it is part of their country. They therefore refuse to discuss the Orontes with Turkey since this could be construed as tacit recognition of Turkish sovereignty over the Hatay." *See* Shapland, *supra* note 98, at 146.

the Project provided the Bank with the opportunity to hold extensive internal deliberations on how to deal with projects on international rivers. Fuelled by Turkey's objection, those deliberations resulted in paving the way for the issuance of the first Bank policy for dealing with projects on shared watercourses.

4.3 *Operational Memorandum 8, 1956*

The first World Bank policy dealing with projects on shared watercourses was issued on 6 March 1956 as Operational Memorandum No. 8 (OM 8) and was entitled "Projects on International Inland Waterways."[105] The fact that this Operational Memorandum was number 8, which meant that it was preceded by a few other operational memoranda, and that it was issued less than 10 years after the Bank started its lending operations, underscored the urgency of the issues surrounding World Bank financed projects on international waterways.

The OM emphasized the fact that projects on international inland waterways are likely to give rise to problems that go far beyond the usual problems of project analysis in that they could affect relations not only between the Bank and its borrowers, but also among governments. The OM went on to state that these projects need special handling.

However, the OM did not set forth any substantive rules for handling these projects. Instead, paragraph 1 of the OM stated that it was "vital that the Bank decide how each case will be handled before discussions have reached a stage at which it would be embarrassing to introduce new questions." Accordingly, the OM confirmed the 'flexible approach' where the facts and circumstances of each proposed project would determine how the Bank would handle that project. It also provided the basis for dispute avoidance, which has become one major aspect of the Bank policies, procedures, and operations. OM 8 has seven main features.

First, it enumerated the types of projects covered, which included hydroelectric, irrigation, flood control, navigation, drainage or similar projects. The term 'similar projects' was meant to give flexibility to the Bank to include projects not enumerated in the OM, but which could affect the international waterway in question.

Second, the OM also went beyond the term 'international rivers' used by the Bank prior to the OM being issued. As may be noted, the international waters issues that the Bank faced until that time all related to shared rivers, and the Bank had not been faced with issues of transboundary lakes. Yet, OM 8 used the term 'international inland waterways' as the title of the OM.

105 The OM 8 was approved by the World Bank Loan Committee on 8 February 1956. A copy of the OM is attached as Appendix 1 to Salman *The World Bank Policy*, *supra* note 86.

Third, it is worth noting that the OM chose the term 'waterways' over the term 'watercourses' used by the IIL in the Madrid Declaration. It should be added that the first international instruments to use the term waterways was the Barcelona Convention, which is titled 'Convention and Statute on the Regime of Navigable Waterways of International Concern.'[106] As noted below, this term continues to be used in all successive policies for projects on shared watercourses issued by the Bank.

Fourth, the OM defined international inland waterways to include a river, canal, lake or other inland waterway "which forms a boundary between or flows through two or more countries." Accordingly, the OM made it clear that the definition included successive rivers, as well as boundary rivers and lakes.

Fifth, the countries sharing the waterways did not need to be members of the Bank. Paragraph 2(a) of the OM extended its application to all riparians of the shared inland waterway, "whether members or non-members of the Bank." This is an interesting, albeit necessary, feature of the OM. It went beyond the responsibilities of the Bank to all its members under the Articles of Agreement and emphasized application of the OM to non-member riparian states as well. This approach was considered necessary because of the general obligation under international law to avoid harm to all other riparians, which is a basic obligation that the Bank could not possibly overlook. By making an explicit reference to non-members, the Bank was simply emphasizing and underscoring this obligation. This emphasis on the application of the policy to non-members of the Bank would remain as one of the main features in all subsequent Bank policies for projects on international waterways. It is worth adding that the Bank membership had grown from 38 countries in 1946, to 58 in 1956.[107]

Sixth, the OM did not set forth any specific policies or substantive rules and procedures to be followed for these projects with regards to the prospective borrower and the other riparians. Rather, it stated that if the project was covered by the OM, then:

> (b) … the management should be informed promptly, and the Working Party for the project and the interested department should make it their first order of business to propose and obtain management approval of a procedure for dealing with the international aspects of the project.

106 *See supra* note 64.

107 For the membership of the Bank in 1956, *see* International Bank for Reconstruction and Development, *Eleventh Annual Report 1955–1956* (Washington, DC: The World Bank, 1956), at 27.

> (c) No steps should be taken to investigate the merits of the project or to process the project without prior approval from the management. This requirement is to be observed even if the international aspects appear to be covered by international agreement, or if there appears to be *prima facie* evidence that the project cannot be adversely affected by, or will not adversely affect, up-stream or down-stream riparian states.[108]

The fact that the OM did not include any specific policies or procedures, but left it to the Working Party to propose and obtain management approval for such procedures indicated that the Bank had decided to follow the "flexible approach" discussed above, and to deal with each project based on its facts and circumstances. It is worth noting that the requirement of proposing and obtaining management approval of a procedure for dealing with the project applied to cases where the issues were covered by an international agreement. The requirement also applied to cases where there might be *prima facie* evidence that the project could not be adversely affected by, or would not adversely affect, upstream or downstream riparian states. In this way, the OM left no exceptions for cases where the Working Party could proceed with the project before informing Bank management and receiving its instructions as to how to handle the issues related to the international waterway under the proposed project.

Seventh, as indicated above, the OM addressed both situations: the project not being adversely affected by, or adversely affecting, upstream or downstream riparian states.[109] This statement raises two issues:

The first is whether the Bank was concerned only with adverse effects on downstream riparians by upstream riparians, or whether it contemplated that downstream riparians could also affect upstream riparians. It is interesting that the deliberations within the Bank prior to the issuance of the OM raised the possibility that Bank-financed projects could assist borrowers in establishing water rights that could be later claimed as established or acquired rights. The establishment of water rights and claiming them later as acquired rights basically relates to the potential foreclosure of future uses of such waters, as discussed above.[110] This concept fosters the argument that downstream riparians can adversely affect upstream riparians by foreclosing the future uses of the waters of the shared river. It may not be easy to argue that this concept was fully comprehended at that time by Bank staff and

108 OM 8, *supra* note 105, paras. 2(b) and (c).

109 *Id.*, para. 2(c).

110 *See* Salman, *supra* note 18.

management, and that it was indeed intended by the above paragraph in the OM. However, the deliberations as well as the content of the OM indicate that the issue was being thought about.

The second issue related to the notion that a project may be adversely affected by the other riparians. The most likely possibility in this connection is that future projects in one upstream riparian may affect Bank-financed projects in a downstream riparian, such as by decreasing the water flow to this downstream riparian. This situation can only be dealt with by trying to ascertain the intentions and plans of those upstream riparians. Ascertaining such intentions is not a simple task, and it may not be easy to undertake given that such riparians would be under no obligation to disclose their future plans, even if they had prepared such plans. However, regardless of how simple or difficult it could be to ascertain the intentions of other riparians, this task can only be achieved through notification of these other riparians.

Thus, the OM, and the flexible approach it adopted, set in motion a process of notification of the other riparians of Bank-financed projects on international waterways. This process has resulted in extensive and rich legal literature in the field which has been influenced by the existing and emerging principles of international water law, and in turn contributed to the evolution and progressive development of those principles.

There is no doubt that OM 8 was a major milestone in the operational work of the Bank in the field of shared waterways. It is true that the OM did not include any substantive principles and policies for dealing with the intricate issues posed by projects on international waterways. However, the OM underscored the obligation of the Bank to avoid disputes and to seek an approach for dealing with the international aspects of a project that takes into account the interests of all the riparians. The Bank itself had by that time elaborated a number of possible approaches for dealing with each project. As Raj Krishna noted, the OM "established an early warning system by requiring the Bank's management to be informed promptly of any project which involved the use of an international watercourse. No steps were to be taken to investigate the merits, or process a project without management approval of a procedure for dealing with the international aspects of the project."[111] The different approaches proposed and followed by the Bank for the varying projects that the Bank financed on international waterways gradually constituted the building blocks for the evolution of the successive Bank policies in this field, with notification being the central element of these policies.

---

111 Krishna, *'The Evolution and Context of the Bank Policy'*, *supra* note 94, at 32–33.

4.4 *Operational Memorandum 5.05, 1965*

Operational Memorandum No. 8, issued on 6 March 1956, continued in force until it was replaced by Operational Memorandum 5.05 which was issued on 1 January 1965.[112] A number of factors prompted the Bank to undertake the revisions to OM 8. Membership of the Bank had increased considerably from 58 members in 1956, to 103 in 1965.[113] This followed attainment of independence by many countries, particularly in Africa, many of which joined the World Bank immediately thereafter. Most of those countries were attracted to the Bank by, *inter alia*, the economic and sector work undertaken by the Bank, as well as the interest-free credits provided by the Bank under the new window of the International Development Association (IDA).[114]

Thus, more new member countries, with a large number of shared watercourses, and with varying projects on these shared watercourses resulted in more challenges that required attention. OMS 5.05 introduced a number of changes to OM 8. Those changes can be summarized as follows:

First, the title of the OM was changed. The previous title of OM 8 "Projects on International Inland Waterways" was replaced by the title "Projects on International Waters." This change was prompted by the inclusion of a new paragraph, discussed below, adding a new category of international waterways comprising bays, gulfs, straits, and channels to the waterways already covered under OM 8. As such, the 1965 OM no longer dealt only with inland waterways such as rivers, lakes, and canals. Its scope was expanded to include semi-enclosed coastal waters such as bays, gulfs, straits, and channels. Thus, both inland waters as well as semi-enclosed coastal waters were covered under the 1965 OM. This change, in turn, resulted in a new title to the 1965 OM to encompass both types of waterways.

Second, the list of projects enumerated in the 1965 OM included two new types of projects – sewage and industrial projects – in addition to those included in the 1956 OM.[115] This was the result of expansion of the scope of the projects that the Bank started financing.

---

112 OM 5.05 is attached as Appendix 2 to Salman, *The World Bank Policy, supra* note 86.

113 For the membership of the Bank in 1956, *see supra* note 107. For the membership in 1965, *see* International Bank for Reconstruction and Development and International Development Association, *1965–1966 Annual Report* (Washington, DC: The World Bank, 1966), at 24.

114 *See supra* note 19.

115 The list of the projects enumerated in paragraph (b)(i) of OM 5.05 included "hydroelectric, irrigation, flood control, navigation, drainage, sewage, industrial or similar project."

Third, the effects of the proposed projects extended from use of the waters to include pollution of those waters. As such, both water quantity as well as quality issues were included in the 1965 OM.

Fourth, a new paragraph 2 was added. This paragraph stated that the procedures set forth in the preceding paragraph should also be followed in the case of any project involving such international waters as bays, gulfs, straits, or channels bound by several states or, if within one state, recognized as necessary channels of communication between the open sea and other states. This paragraph basically added semi-enclosed coastal waters to the policy. The addition of such waters to inland waterways may seem confusing – mixing freshwater and sea water.

The 1956 OM was meant to address the pressing and complex issues of projects on shared rivers and lakes. A number of those rivers and lakes had been characterized by the competing demands of the different riparian states. The Bank policy for projects on international inland waterways was meant to ensure that the Bank would act prudently in the interests of all the states concerned, and try to avoid projects that may result in disputes, or exacerbate existing ones. Thus, the immediate question that arises is what prompted the Bank to add semi-enclosed coastal waters to its policy on inland waters, and what purpose was the new addition expected to serve?

The Bank had by the early 1960s started financing navigation,[116] industrial, and sewage projects. The latter two types of projects were added to the list of projects in the 1965 OM. These projects could affect the quality of the waters of bays, gulfs, straits, or channels by polluting such waters. Accordingly, the concern was more on quality, than quantity. The Bank wanted to ensure that the projects it planned to finance would not adversely affect the quality of the waters of those bays, gulfs, straits, and channels, and that this determination was shared by the states concerned.

It should be recalled that when the semi-enclosed coastal waters were included in the 1965 OM, the Bank still did not have a policy on the environment; the first such policy was issued in 1984.[117] Obviously these types of waters and projects are best dealt with through an EIA, which would identify any adverse impacts caused by the project and recommend ways for mitigating such impacts, and not through the policy for projects on international waterways.

---

116 It should be clarified that that the Bank considers navigation projects to include not only the construction of ports, but also the financing of ships, as indicated in the various projects that the Bank finances in this area; *see* Salman, *The World Bank Policy*, *supra* note 86.

117 The first policy on the environment was issued by the World Bank in 1984 as OMS 2.36; *see* Salman, *id.*, at 32.

However, it seems that since the Bank did not have a policy on the environment in 1965, semi-enclosed coastal waters were added to the policy on inland waterways.

One possible justification given for adding these types of waters was dispute avoidance among the littoral states, as well as between the Bank and those states, on the issue of the pollution of these waters through Bank-financed project. Disputes have arisen among a number of countries on the boundaries of their semi-enclosed coastal waters, and financing projects that might affect them was bound to exacerbate these disputes.[118] As will be discussed below, those types of semi-enclosed coastal waters continue to be part of the Bank policy for projects on international waterways even after the Bank adopted detailed policies on environmental assessment. Moreover, the scope of these types of waters has been expanded.

The 1965 OM also included a new paragraph concerning the presentation of loans and/or credits to the Executive Directors of the Bank and IDA. The paragraph stated that:

> when presenting loan or credit projects on international waters to the Executive Directors, both the Appraisal Report and the Report and Recommendation of the President should state that the Bank/IDA has considered the international aspects of the project and is satisfied that:
> (i) the issues involved are covered by appropriate arrangements between the borrower and other riparians; or
> (ii) the other riparians have stated (to the borrower or to the Bank/IDA) that they have no objection to the project; or
> (iii) the project is not harmful to the interests of other riparians, and their absence of express consent is immaterial or their objections are not justified.[119]

This paragraph added substantive elements to the basic procedural rules included in OM 8. Henceforth every Bank-financed project on international waters would fall under one of the above three categories. As a first step, the Bank would need to determine if the shared waterway or the project was covered by an agreement between the borrower and the other riparians. If the project was

118 The Gulf of Fonseca is one such example. The Gulf is bounded by El Salvador, Honduras, and Nicaragua. Honduras and Nicaragua had for a long time disputed their maritime boundaries, and the issue had to be settled by the ICJ. *See Case Concerning Territorial and Maritime Dispute between Nicaragua and Honduras in the Caribbean Sea (Nicaragua v. Honduras)*, Judgement of 8 October 1997, ICJ Reports 2007, 659.

119 OM 5.05, *supra* note 112, para. 3.

not covered by such an agreement, then those riparians would have to convey to the borrower or the Bank their no-objection to the project. Although the OM did not require notification explicitly, there was no way for the other riparians to give no-objection to the project unless they were already notified. Thus, notification was clearly underscored by the 1965 OM.

The third step proposed by the 1965 OM would have to follow as a result of the notification: receipt of an objection (termed as absence of express consent) that would not be justified. Thus, if the Bank had determined that the project was not harmful to the interests of the riparians, then the absence of express consent would be immaterial, and the objection would not be justified. In this way the Bank became the final arbiter of the differences in opinion between the other riparians on the effects of the project on the shared waterway.

This third step codified the Bank's earlier approach of not financing projects that could cause adverse effects to the other riparians. The 1965 OM used the phrase "harmful to the interests of other riparians," which is not different in substance from "will not adversely affect" also used in the OM itself.[120] Henceforth, the Bank approach to projects on international waterways would highlight the obligation to notify other riparian states of projects on shared waterways even if the project would not cause harm to any of them. Harm, as the Bank policy prescribed, could be quantitative, or qualitative, or both.[121]

Subsequently, notification of other riparians of the proposed project started to become a basic and cardinal component of Bank-financed projects on international waterways. No doubt, this was a major milestone in the evolution of the Bank policy, and a significant step in clarifying the hitherto uncodified Bank policy with regards to notification.

One ensuing question that could arise relates to how the Bank would handle an objection from one or more riparians. The OM was silent on this issue. It seemed that the Bank intentionally left this issue unaddressed so that it would deal with such objections on a case-by-case basis, depending on the nature of the project and the objection.[122]

Thus, it can be concluded that the issue of how to deal with projects on shared watercourses occupied the attention of the World Bank from the early days of the commencement of its operational work. The principles of international water law were at the infancy stage at that time; yet, the Bank started recognizing the need for notifying all other riparians of such projects from

120 *Id.*, paras. 1 (b)(ii) and 3.

121 *See* Salman, *The World Bank Policy*, *supra* note 86.

122 The issue of objection to the planned measure by one or more of the riparians is discussed in detail in part 7 of this monograph.

the start. This requirement was necessitated and bolstered by the nature of the World Bank as an international cooperative financial institution.

Although the 1956 OM did not include explicit provisions on notification, it required ascertaining the intentions of other riparians; a task that can only be achieved through notification of these riparians. Similarly, the 1965 OM did not include an explicit provision on the notification requirement. However, the OM required the staff to certify, *inter alia*, that the project is not harmful to the interests of other riparians, and their absence of express consent is immaterial, or their objections are not justified. Consent of other riparians, or the absence of their consent, or the determination that the objection is not justified, can only be ascertained through notification of these riparians. Accordingly, with the issuance of the 1956 OM, and confirmation of its main provisions in the 1965 OM, notification became in practice the main feature of the Bank financed projects on shared waterways.[123]

OM 5.05 of 1965 was reissued in March 1971 as OM 2.22, with no changes to its content. OM 2.22 was again reissued as Operational Manual Statement (OMS) 2.32 in October 1977, with only some nomenclature changes to reflect regional reorganization of the World Bank.[124] Accordingly, the procedural and substantive rules set forth in 1965 in OM 5.05, with notification constituting the main element, would continue to govern the financing of projects on shared watercourses until 1971, when OM 5.05 was replaced by OMS 2.22, and again by OMS 2.32 in 1977. The provisions of OMS 2.32 of 1977 were revised significantly in 1985, with notification taking an explicit and clear centre stage of the Bank policy for projects on shared watercourses, as will be discussed in the next part of this monograph.

Part 5: The World Bank Current Policies and Practice on Notification

5.1 *The Gradual Institutionalization of the Notification Requirement*

As discussed in the previous part of this monograph, during the period 1956 to 1985, the Bank issued a series of policies regarding the processing of projects on shared watercourses. Although each of these policies was more or less a framework that had to be filled by the circumstances surrounding each project, notification of other riparians of the proposed project on the shared watercourse started to become the main feature of the practice of the Bank. This

123 *See* Salman, *The World Bank Policy*, *supra* note 86.

124 *See* Krishna, *International Waters in Bank Projects*, *supra* note 101.

practice of notification prevailed despite the fact that the term 'notification' was not explicitly mentioned under any of the then existing policies.

Notification was undertaken, despite the absence of the term and procedures thereon, through varying ways: by the beneficiary state itself, or by the Bank directly to the other riparians, or through the Executive Director representing each of the other riparians. The notified states would be given a reasonable period of time, varying between two to six months, to reply. However, the number of challenging projects, as well as challenging responses from riparian states to notification, kept rising.

The Bank faced a major challenge in 1983–1984. In March 1983 the Bank started processing the Igdir-Aksu-Eregli-Ercis Irrigation Project (hereinafter Igdir-Aksu Project, or the Project) in Turkey on the Aras River, which Turkey shares with Iran and, at that time, the Union of Soviet Socialist Republics (USSR or Soviet Union). The Project involved the financing of four irrigation sub-projects that were expected to bring about 113,000 hectares of dry land or inadequately irrigated areas under improved irrigation.[125] The Project included, *inter alia*, the construction of additional irrigation canals, intakes, drainage works, and rehabilitation and improvement of an existing irrigation and drainage system. One of the sub-projects, the Igdir sub-project, involved utilization of water from the Aras River. This River formed at that time the border between Turkey and the Soviet Union, and further downstream, formed the border between the USSR and Iran.

A convention (with a protocol attached thereto) concluded in 1927 between Turkey and the USSR[126] was considered by the Bank to be a satisfactory arrangement for the Project, and hence the USSR was not notified of the Project.[127] However, Iran was not a party to this convention or any other agreement on

125 Turkey, Igdir-Aksu-Eregli-Ercis (IAEE) Irrigation Project (P008950, 1984).

126 Convention and Protocol between the Union of Soviet Socialist Republics and Turkey regarding the Use of Frontier Waters, Kars, 8 January 1927; 926, 127 British and Foreign State Papers 1927 (H. M. Stationary Office, 1932).

127 There were some views within the Bank that even if the Bank had concluded that the Convention was not a satisfactory arrangement for the Project, the USSR would not have been notified of the Project because it was not a member of the Bank at that time. Those views were based on the premise that the Bank only needed to ensure that the Project would not cause appreciable harm to a non-member, and that there was no notification requirement. However, other views were voiced that the Bank should ensure that all the riparians, whether members of the Bank or not, and whether there was a satisfactory agreement or not, were notified because this is an established requirement under international water law. Thus, the issue of notification of non-members was not fully resolved.

the Aras River with Turkey, although Iran had concluded an agreement in 1957 with the USSR on the Aras River.[128]

Bank staff was of the opinion that the storage of additional water from the Aras River for the Igdir sub-project would not have any significant adverse effects on Iran. These findings were conveyed to Iran, and at first no response was received from Iran. However, the Executive Director representing Iran requested that consideration of the proposed project by the Executive Directors of the Bank scheduled for 9 June 1983, be postponed until 14 June 1983. Iran claimed that the Project might have a detrimental effect on Iran, and asked for further information and technical data. At the meeting on 14 June, the Executive Directors decided to defer consideration of the proposed project for another month, until July 12, in order to allow the Government of Iran more time to examine the technical data on the Project.

Meanwhile, the Iranian government reiterated concerns that the Project would adversely affect operation of one of its dams on the Aras River during possible drought. The Iranian government proposed that consideration of the Project should be postponed until a trilateral commission consisting of Iran, the USSR, and Turkey had reviewed the Project. While the proposal of a trilateral commission was rejected, consideration of the Project by the Executive Directors was further delayed. Iran continued to insist that the Project would cause adverse effects to its interests. Iran asked for more information, which was provided, and the date of consideration of the Project of 4 October 1983 was postponed further. By that time Bank staff reconfirmed that there would be no adverse effects on Iran,[129] and recommended proceeding with the processing of the proposed project under paragraph 4(c) of OMS 2.32, which stated that

128 Agreement between Iran and the Union of Soviet Socialist Republics for the Joint Utilization of the Frontier Parts of the Aras and Atrak for Irrigation and Generation of Power, Tehran, 11 August 1957; 428, 163 British and Foreign State Papers, 1957–58, (H. M. Stationary Office, 1966).

129 The main issue for Iran was that the Project would cause a slight (on average, about three percent) reduction in energy production, particularly in years of low river flows. Bank staff believed that reduction to be acceptable for two reasons. First, it was only a small proportion of the energy production from the Aras Hydropower Project and Iran's economic benefits from the river (i.e., about 0.3 percent of total economic benefits). At that time, about 10 percent of Iran's economic benefits from the Aras River waters came from power production and 90 percent from irrigation. The second reason was that the reduction in energy production in Iran, due to Turkey proposing to use part of its reasonable and equitable share of the Aras River waters, was fully predictable by Iran at the time of the construction of the original Aras Project, as it had been predicted for subsequent projects.

"the project is not harmful to the interests of other riparians and their absence of express consent is immaterial or their objections are not justified."

Nonetheless, correspondence between the Bank and Iran continued, and a Bank mission visited Iran in April 1984 to discuss the Project and Iran's objection. The Project was finally presented to and approved by the Executive Directors on 5 June 1984, one year after the original date planned for its presentation. The approval was part of a compromise that was proposed by the Executive Director for Iran. The compromise consisted of three elements: (i) approval of the project as presented by Bank management; (ii) use by Bank management of its good offices to promote an agreement between Turkey and Iran over the Aras River; and (iii) preparation by Bank management of a paper for the purposes of review of the present guidelines for projects on international waters. The latter element was included because several Executive Directors recognized that the Bank policies and practice for projects on shared watercourses in force at that time were not adequate to deal with the complex issues of notification and the responses thereto, as demonstrated by projects like the Igdir-Aksu Project.

Accordingly, it took one full year to deal with the objections of Iran to the Project, and Iran's challenges to the Bank staff determination that the project would not cause adverse effects to its interests.[130] The Project was repeatedly taken off the agenda of the Executive Directors of the Bank, and more data and information was requested by, and supplied to Iran. Turkey assisted in supplying such data and information, but kept pressing for presentation of the Project to the Executive Directors. As a result, the Bank became an arbiter in the dispute over the Project and its impacts, and the process gradually turned into negotiations over larger issues, not just the Project, namely the Aras River, and the Bank policy for projects on international waters. The Bank also became acutely aware that its policies for projects on shared watercourses needed to be revised to handle the complex issue of notification and its results.

The Bank took some initial steps to use its good offices to promote an agreement between Iran and Turkey over the Aras River, but no such agreement was reached. The issues concerning the Aras River were quite complex. One complicating factor was the fact that the USSR was also a riparian, indeed a major riparian, of the Aras River. The USSR was not a member of the Bank, and the

130 As mentioned above, the initial date set for consideration of the Project by the Bank Executive Directors was 14 June 1983. The Project was finally considered and approved by the Executive Directors on 5 June 1984, one year from the initial date.

Bank had no leverage over, or dealings with the USSR at that time.[131] As such, it was not possible for the Bank to approach and effectively involve the USSR. Accordingly, the Bank's efforts in this aspect did not go far.[132] However, Iran did get Bank management to prepare a memorandum on the implementation of its policy for projects on international waters, and to recommend major revisions to the policies and procedures that governed Bank-financed projects on international waterways.

5.2 *Operational Manual Statement 2.32, 1985*

In response to the Executive Directors' discussion and decision on 5 June 1984, a memorandum entitled "Riparian Rights: The Bank Experience – Staff Review and Recommendations" was prepared by Bank management.[133] The memorandum was discussed and approved by the Executive Directors on 7 March 1985. The memorandum included four parts. Part I dealt with the main characteristics of, and statistics on, water resources, and the global supply and demand situation. Part II surveyed the basic principles of international water law prevailing at that time. Part III dealt with the Bank policy and practice with regards to projects on international waters since the Bank started to finance such projects. Finally, Part IV presented the recommendation section of the memorandum, and included the detailed proposed changes to the then existing policies and procedures (OMS 2.32 of October 1977). Based on the recommendations approved by the Executive Directors on 7 March 1985, a new and more detailed and comprehensive OMS 2.32 was issued in April 1985.[134]

It is worth noting that the first Operational Memorandum for Projects on Inland International Waterways (OM 8 of 1956) was issued as a result of the objection of Turkey to the Ghab Project in Syria. The OMS 2.32 of 1985 was issued as a result of the objection of Iran to the Igdir-Aksu Project in Turkey and the specific request of Iran that revised guidelines for projects on international

131 The Russian Federation joined the World Bank in 1992, following the collapse of the Union of Soviet Socialist Republics (USSR) in 1991. Other former countries of the Soviet Union followed suit.

132 It could also be argued that the circumstances surrounding the objection, and later the approval of the Project by the Executive Directors, were perhaps additional factors for the Bank's efforts not to go far in this aspect.

133 Memorandum R85-16, IDA/R85-6, dated 17 January 1985. The Committee that prepared the Memorandum was chaired by Dr. Raj Krishna to whom this monograph is dedicated. The reader will also find other reports and publications by Dr. Krishna on the subject matter, referred to in this monograph, and listed in its Bibliography.

134 For a copy of OMS 2.32 of 1985, *see* Salman, *The World Bank Policy*, *supra* note 86, Appendix 3.

waterways be issued. As will be discussed below, addition by the Bank of transboundary groundwater to the definition of international waterways, and thus application of the Policy to transboundary groundwater, resulted from a project in Algeria. The Middle East and North Africa region had at that time, and still has, the lowest per capita net water distribution in the world.[135] Although the region is home to five percent of the world's population, it contains less than one percent of the world's annual renewable freshwater.[136] Thus, it should not come as a surprise that the countries of the region have been overzealous in protecting their interests and what they see as their water security in the shared watercourses in the region.

The OMS that was issued in April 1985 drew substantially from the principles of international water law established or emerging at that time. It should be recalled that, by the time the new Policy was approved in 1985, a number of rules dealing with international watercourses had been adopted, including the Helsinki Rules, which were issued by the International Law Association in 1966.[137] It should also be added that the International Law Commission had already started working on a draft watercourses convention in 1971, and had, by the time the Bank prepared its 1985 Policy, issued a number of reports.[138] In addition, the new Policy drew substantially from the Bank experience with projects on international waterways over the course of its operation during the past 40 years (since it started operations in 1946).[139]

The 1985 OMS underwent minor changes, and was reissued in 1990 as Operational Directive (OD 7.50). This OD was reissued in 2001 as Operational Policy and Bank Procedures – OP and BP 7.50 (in addition to Good Practice –

135 The World Bank, *Making the Most of Scarcity, Accountability for Better Water Management in the Middle East and North Africa* (Washington, DC: The World Bank, 2007), at 4. The Report states: "Per capita renewable water resources in the region, which in 1950 were 4,000 m per year, are currently 1,100 m per year. Projections indicate that they will drop by half, reaching 550 m per person in 2050. This compares to a global average of 8,900 m per person per year today, and about 6,000 m per person in 2050 when the world population will reach more than 9 billion." *Id.*, at 5.

136 *See* The World Bank, *From Scarcity to Security – Averting a Water Crisis in the Middle East and North Africa* (Washington, DC: The World Bank, 1998).

137 *See* ILA, *Report of the Fifty-Second Conference*, *supra* note 45.

138 As indicated above, the UNGA asked the ILC in 1970 to study the topic of 'international watercourses' and prepare a draft convention. The ILC started its work on the draft convention in 1971.

139 *See* R. Krishna, *'International Watercourses: World Bank Experience and Policy'*, in J. A. Allan & C. Mallat (eds.), *Water in the Middle East: Legal, Political and Commercial Implications* (I. B. Tauris Publishers, 1995).

GP 7.50).[140] Both the OP and BP were reissued in March 2012 to reflect the current organizational structure of the Bank. The 2012 versions of the OP and BP are still in force and effect.[141]

As indicated above, attempts have been underway for aligning the Policy with the UN Watercourses Convention with regards to establishing a threshold for notification, but these attempts have been sidelined by work on the new Environment and Social Framework (ESF).[142] It should also be reiterated that the policy has not been affected by the 2016 changes to the environmental and social safeguard policies and the adoption of the new set of the Environmental and Social Standards.[143]

5.3 *Types of International Waterways Covered under the Policy*

Paragraph 1 of OP 7.50 states that the Policy applies to the following types of international waterways:

(a) any river, canal, lake, or similar body of water that forms a boundary between, or any river or body of surface water that flows through, two or more states, whether Bank members or not;

(b) any tributary or other body of surface water that is a component of any waterway described in (a) above; and

(c) any bay, gulf, strait, or channel bounded by two or more states or, if within one state, recognized as a necessary channel of communication between the open sea and other states – and any river flowing into such waters.

Thus, the Policy continues using the term 'waterways.' It continues to define the term in such a way to include not only shared freshwaters, but also semi-enclosed coastal waters. Such coastal waters could be bounded by two or more states. They could also fall within one state, but in such a case, they should be recognized as a necessary channel of communication between the open sea and other states.[144] The definition also includes rivers flowing into any of the semi-enclosed coastal waters covered by the Policy. The reference here

140 A copy of the 1990 OD is reproduced as Appendix 4 in Salman, *The World Bank Policy*, *supra* note 86. 2001 The 2001 version of the OP is reproduced as Appendix 5A; of the BP as Appendix 5B; and the GP as Appendix 5C, in Salman, *id.*

141 The version of OP 7.50, as revised in March 2012, is available at: https://policies.worldbank.org/sites/ppf3/PPFDocuments/Forms/DispPage.aspx?docid=2660.
The version of BP 7.50, as revised in March 2012, is available at: https://policies.worldbank.org/sites/ppf3/PPFDocuments/Forms/DispPage.aspx?docid=1843.

142 *Supra* note 25.

143 *Supra* note 27.

144 As an example, this would include in the definition the Strait of Bosporus and the Sea of Marmara in Turkey since they are recognized as the only channels of communication between a number of states (the other Black Sea states) and the Mediterranean Sea.

clearly is to national rivers. Such rivers have been included in the definition of 'international waterways' by virtue of their emptying into semi-enclosed international waters.

Poor and improper uses of such national rivers could adversely affect those semi-enclosed coastal waters, and this in turn could adversely affect other states. However, it should be clarified that the Policy deals with the qualitative aspects of the waters of those types of waterways, while in the case of rivers and lakes, both quantitative and qualitative aspects are covered by the Policy. Furthermore, OP 7.50 states that the Policy applies regardless of whether the states sharing the waterway are Bank members or not.

Another observation about the definition of international waterways under the Policy is that it does not include shared groundwater. The drafters of the Policy felt, at the time the Policy was being prepared in 1984–1985, that not enough technical information was available to assist with the inclusion of shared groundwater.[145] However, soon after the Policy was adopted, the Bank financed a project involving the use of transboundary groundwater in Algeria in 1990, and the General Counsel at that time instructed application of the Policy provisions to transboundary groundwater.[146] Those instructions have

145 It should be clarified that the 1966 Helsinki Rules, *supra* note 45, did include transboundary groundwater connected to surface water. However, in 1986, the ILA issued the Seoul Rules which extended application of the Helsinki Rules to aquifers that do not receive water from, or contribute water to, surface water. With regards to the Watercourses Convention, after the ILC completed the work on the draft Watercourses Convention in 1994, including only transboundary groundwater connected to surface water, it passed a resolution recommending treatment of all types of aquifers in the manner elaborated in the Convention. For more analysis of this matter, and discussion of the resolution, *see* R. Krishna & S. M. A. Salman, *'International Groundwater Law and the World Bank Policy for Projects on Transboundary Groundwater'*, in Salman (ed.), *Groundwater*, *supra* note 51, 163–189.

146 The Sahara Regional Development Project in Algeria (P004938, 1991) was the first project in which the policy on international waterways was extended to transboundary groundwater. The Project involved the utilization of waters by Algeria from two aquifers through the drilling of wells and provision of related equipment and installations, and closure of deteriorating and non-operational wells. One of the aquifers, known as the 'Continental Interclaire', holds fossil, non-renewable waters. The other aquifer, which is known as the 'Complex Terminal', is a rechargeable aquifer. While it has been established by geological studies that these aquifers extend from Algeria to Tunisia, the possibility of their extending further east to Libya and west to Morocco has been indicated by diagrams in some reports. An area of about 800,000 cubic kilometers of these aquifers has been studied by the United Nations Educational, Scientific and Cultural Organization during the period 1968–1971, with funding from the United Nations Development Programme (UNDP), as part of a strategy to explore water resources in the desert areas of the world. The studies were undertaken with the intention of assessing the water resources potential in these

since been followed, and the Policy continues to be applied to transboundary groundwater, as happened with the Disi Aquifer.[147] To date, no amendment has been introduced to the definition of the term international waterways to include an explicit reference to transboundary groundwater.

It should be noted in this connection that a number of international legal instruments, such as the UN Watercourse Convention, define international watercourses to include transboundary groundwater. However, like the Helsinki Rules, the UN Watercourses Convention applies only to "a system of surface waters and groundwaters constituting by virtue of their physical relationship a unitary whole and normally flowing into a common terminus." Accordingly, the Convention does not extend to aquifers that do not receive water from, or contribute water to surface waters, namely fossil aquifers.[148] These are the

---

areas and to propose a policy for their exploitation by both Algeria and Tunisia. In 1983 UNDP reviewed and updated this study. For more discussion, *see* Krishna & Salman, *supra* note 145; *see* also http://www.internationalwatersgovernance.com/north-western-sahara-aquifer-system-nwsas.html.

147 The Bank faced the issue of transboundary groundwater again in 1997, a few years after the Sahara Regional Development Project. This time it was the Disi-Amman Water Conveyor Project. Under the proposed Project, Jordan would convey water from the Disi aquifer to Amman through a 350-kilometer conveyor. The Disi Aquifer is a fossil, non-renewable aquifer that underlies both northern Saudi Arabia and southern Jordan. However, no agreement or joint management mechanism for the aquifer existed between the two countries at that time. The proposed Project would abstract up to 100 million cubic meters a year (MCM/yr), with the likelihood that the figure may climb to 150 MCM/yr to meet the growing demand for water in Amman. The well-fields to be drilled would be about 35 kilometers from the borders with Saudi Arabia. Although the Bank took note of the fact that OP/BP 7.50, *supra* note 141, refers only to surface water, the precedent of the Sahara Regional Development Project in Algeria was considered. It was decided that the precedent should be followed. Accordingly, the Bank informed Jordan of the need to notify Saudi Arabia of the Project. For a detailed discussion of the Project, *see* A. Macoun & H. El Naser, *'Groundwater Resources Management in Jordan: Policy and Regulatory Issues'*, in Salman (ed.), *Groundwater*, *supra* note 51, at 105.

148 *See* G. Eckstein, *'A Hydrological Perspective of the Status of Ground Water Resources Under the UN Watercourse Convention'*, 30 Columbia Journal of Environmental Law (2005) 525–564. Other instruments dealing with transboundary groundwater include the 1991 Espoo Convention, *supra* note 56, and the 1992 Helsinki Convention, *supra* note 58. The Espoo Convention requires notification of other riparian states in cases where the annual volume of water to be abstracted from the shared aquifer by one state amounts to 10 million cubic meters or more. It should be added that the ILC has prepared the Draft Articles on the Law of Transboundary Aquifers. The Draft Articles are modeled on the UN Watercourses Convention and includes provisions on notification of planned activities that may have significant adverse effect on other aquifer states. The Draft Articles covers all types of groundwater – fossil aquifers as well as aquifers connected to surface waters. *See also* G. Eckstein, *The International Law of Transboundary Groundwater Resources* (Routledge, 2017).

kinds of aquifers to which the World Bank extended application of its Policy, as discussed above.

The Bank Policy continues to apply to shared watercourses, as well as to semi-enclosed coastal waters. Inclusion of semi-enclosed coastal waters continued despite the fact that the Bank has issued strict and comprehensive policies on the environment that would certainly cover such waters. However, it has been argued that the purpose behind inclusion by the Bank of semi-enclosed coastal waters in its Policy for projects on international waterways is to ensure that the concerned states are notified of any project that may affect them and are given an opportunity to voice any concerns they may have on such a project.

5.4 *Types of Projects Covered under the Policy*

Paragraph 2 of OP 7.50 states that the Policy applies to the following types of projects:

(a) hydroelectric, irrigation, flood control, navigation, drainage, water and sewerage, industrial, and similar projects that involve the use or potential pollution of international waterways; and

(b) detailed design and engineering studies of projects under para. (a) above, including those to be carried out by the Bank as executing agency or in any other capacity.

The Policy enumerates the projects that are to be covered, and such projects include not only projects involving installations and works, but also other types of projects such as navigation. Also included are detailed design and engineering studies for the enumerated projects. As an international cooperative financial institution, the Bank believes it is appropriate to include those types of detailed design and engineering studies and extend application of the notification requirement to them, because such design and studies are likely to lead to investment projects. It would be helpful for the Bank, as well as the riparians, to address any questions or differences on the proposed project at the design stage.

5.5 *Policy Basis – Riparian Cooperation*

The Policy states that the Bank, as an international cooperative financial institution

> recognizes that cooperation and goodwill of all the riparian states is essential for the efficient utilization and protection of international waterways. Therefore, the Bank attaches great importance to riparians' making appropriate agreements or arrangements for these purposes for the entire

> waterway or any part thereof. In cases where differences remain unresolved between the state proposing the project and the other riparians, prior to financing the project, the Bank normally urges the beneficiary state to offer to negotiate in good faith with the other riparians to reach appropriate agreements or arrangements.[149]

This emphasis on proactive engagement by the Bank to promote riparians' agreement is important, although this task can be extremely complex, costly, labour intensive, long term, and risky, as evidenced by the Bank's work on the Indus, Aral Sea, Mekong and Nile Basins. While this is not the usual Bank operational work, it is a very important focus for the Bank and one that the Bank is uniquely equipped to tackle, due to its convening power and skill sets, and the 'carrot of investments.'[150] Although the experience of the Indus River System showed a marked success for the Bank, other experiences, such as the Nile Basin Initiative, have not yet achieved their goals.

5.6 *Notification under the Policy*

The Policy requires that "the international aspects of a project on an international waterway are dealt with at the earliest possible opportunity in the project cycle."[151] The prospective borrower should notify the other riparians of the proposed project and its details. As will be discussed throughout this part of the monograph, the Bank Policy requires notification from all the riparians and to all the riparians, regardless of whether they are downstream or upstream riparians. This is because harm, as discussed in the previous parts of this monograph, is a two-way matter.[152]

As stated in Paragraph 4 of OP 7.50, the notification contains, to the extent available, sufficient technical specifications, information, and other data (project details) to enable the other riparians to determine as accurately as possible whether the proposed project has the potential for causing appreciable harm through water deprivation (whether actual deprivation as in the case of downstream riparians, or foreclosure of future uses as in the case of upstream riparians, as discussed earlier), or through pollution or otherwise. Riparian states are given a reasonable period, which could range from two to six months (depending on the nature of the project) to reply.

---

149 OP 7.50, *supra* note 141, para. 3.

150 *See* S. Kirmani & G. Le Moigne, *'Fostering Riparian Cooperation in International River Basins: The World Bank at its Best in Development Diplomacy'*, World Bank Technical Paper No. 335 (Washington, DC: The World Bank, 1997).

151 OP 7.50, *supra* note 141, para. 4.

152 *See* Salman, *supra* note 18.

OP 7.50 goes on to state that "[i]f the prospective borrower indicates to the Bank that it does not wish to give notification, normally the Bank itself does so on behalf of the borrower."[153] Absence of friendly relations between some of the riparians to the same watercourse, or the presence of disputes amongst them, are the typical reasons for some borrowers' refusal to notify other riparians. As discussed in part 3 of this monograph, Article 30 of the UN Watercourses Convention deals with this situation and suggests procedures for addressing it. The Article states that when there are serious obstacles to direct contacts between the watercourse states concerned, they shall then fulfil their obligations of cooperation, including notification, through any indirect procedures accepted by them. If the prospective borrower does not wish to give notification and objects to the Bank's doing so, paragraph 4 of OP 7.50 requires the Bank to discontinue processing of the project. This is understandable given the nature of the Bank as an international cooperative financial institution and the need to maintain the good neighbourliness between the riparian states, which is one underlying reason for notification. Thus, notification is undertaken as a general rule by the borrower; the Bank would undertake the notification on behalf of the borrower if the borrower indicates to the Bank that it does not wish to do so, and has no problem with the Bank undertaking the notification on its behalf. In addition to the borrower and the Bank undertaking the notification for projects on international waterways, the Bank has to study and follow riparians' existing agreements and arrangements for notification, as discussed below.

5.7 *Existing Agreements and Arrangements for Notification*

The Policy requires the Bank to ascertain whether the riparians have entered into agreements or arrangements, or have established any institutional framework for the waterway concerned. In such cases the Bank ascertains the scope of the institution's activities and functions, and the status of its involvement in the proposed project, bearing in mind the possible need for notifying the institution.[154] Indeed, a number of treaties have established river or lake basin management organizations as legal entities, and required the riparians to notify those organizations of any proposed works on such shared river or lake.

Some of the river basin organizations (RBOs) would have different authority with regards to notification under the respective legal instrument establishing them. The RBO may have authority under its legal instrument to act and make a determination on the planned measure of which it is being notified on behalf

153 *See* para. 4 of OP 7.50.

154 OP 7.50, *supra* note 141, para. 5.

of the riparian states that are parties to such an instrument. It would convey its reply to the notification on behalf of the riparians. The RBO may only be authorized to act as a recipient of this notification on behalf of the riparian members of the organization, with no mandate to act on their behalf. This RBO would simply pass on the notification to the riparian states and compile their responses and send them to the notifying state or the Bank (if the Bank has undertaken the notification).

One of the earliest treaties to deal with a role for an RBO in notification is the 1964 Convention and Statutes Relating to the Development of the Chad Basin.[155] The Convention established the Lake Chad Basin Commission (LCBC, or the Commission), and entrusted the LCBC with wide authority. The Statutes state:

> The Member States undertake to refrain from adopting, without referring to the Commission beforehand, any measures likely to exert a marked influence either upon the extent of water losses, or upon the form of the annual hydrograph and limnograph and certain other characteristics of the Lake, upon the conditions of their exploitation by other bordering States, upon the sanitary condition of the water resources, or upon the biological characteristics of the fauna and flora of the Basin. In particular, the Member States agree not to undertake in that part of the Basin falling within their jurisdiction any work likely to have a marked influence upon the system of the water courses and level of the Basin without adequate notice and prior consultation with the Commission.[156]

The Bank took note of this requirement under the Convention and Statutes and has been regularly notifying the LCBC of any projects on or likely to affect the Lake Chad Basin. One example was the Chad-Cameroon Petroleum Development and Pipeline Project of which the LCBC was notified, in addition to the notification sent to the riparian states themselves.[157] Similarly, the LCBC

155 Convention and Statutes relating to the Development of the Chad Basin, Fort Lamy, 22 May 1964, available in FAO, *supra* note 53.

156 Statutes, *id.*, art. 5.

157 The Chad Petroleum Development and Pipeline Project (P044305, 2000) was approved in 2000. It consisted of an IBRD loan of US$39.5 million to the Republic of Chad and US$53.4 million to the Republic of Cameroon to finance part of the equity of the Government of Chad in the Tchad Oil Transportation Company, S.A. (TOTCO) and the Cameroon Oil Transportation Company, S.A. (COTCO). It involved drilling of about 300 wells in southern Chad and the construction of a 1,100 km long pipeline, mostly running through Cameroon, and extending into a subsea pipeline for approximately 11 kilometres to an offshore loading facility.

was notified of a number of Bank-financed projects in Nigeria, including the Fadama Projects.[158] In turn, the LCBC has been responding promptly and appropriately to those notifications.

As indicated above, both the 1973 Treaty and the 1975 Treaty between Uruguay and Argentina on the Uruguay River require that notification regarding the construction or modification of channels or other works affecting the River be given to the Administrative Commission established under the Treaty.[159] Along the same lines, the 1980 Convention Creating the Niger Basin Authority (NBA) obliges the nine riparians of the Niger River to keep the Executive Secretary of the NBA informed of all projects and works that they intend to carry out in the basin.[160] The Agreement on the Establishment of the Zambezi Watercourse Commission obliges each of the parties to notify the Commission of any activity on the Zambezi River that may adversely affect the watercourse or any member state, and to provide the Commission with all available data and information with regard thereto.[161]

The International Commission for the Protection of the Danube River (ICPDR, or the Danube Commission), established under the 1994 Convention on Co-operation for the Protection and Sustainable Use of the River Danube (the Danube Convention), requires that the exchange of information and consultation on planned activities be carried out within the framework of the ICPDR.[162] The Framework Convention for the Protection of the Marine

158 *See* Nigeria, Second National Fadama Development Project (P063622, 2003) and Nigeria, Third National Fadama Development Project (Fadama III) (P096572, 2009).

159 *Supra* note 7.

160 Convention Creating the Niger Basin Authority (with Protocol relating to the Development Fund of the Niger Basin) 1980, 1346 U.N.T.S. 208 (1984). Article 4(4) states: "The member States pledge to keep the Executive Secretariat informed of all the projects and works they might intend to carry out in the Basin. Moreover, they pledge not to undertake any work on the portion of the River, its tributaries and sub-tributaries under their territorial jurisdiction which pollute the waters or modify the biological features of the fauna and the flora."

161 Agreement on the Establishment of the Zambezi Watercourse Commission, Kasane, 13 July 2004, art. 16, available at: http://www.zambezicommission.org/publication/zamcom-agreement.

162 Article 11 of the Danube Convention states: "Having had a prior exchange of information, the Contracting Parties involved shall, at the request of one or several Contracting Parties concerned, enter into consultations on planned activities as referred to in Article 3, paragraph 2, which are likely to cause transboundary impacts, as far as this exchange of information and these consultations are not yet covered by bilateral or other international cooperation. The consultations are carried out as a rule in the framework of the International Commission, with the aim to achieve a solution." The Danube Convention was signed on 29 June 1994, in Sofia, Bulgaria, by 11 of the Danube riparian states (Austria, Bulgaria, Croatia, the Czech Republic, Germany, Hungary, Moldova, Romania, Slovakia,

Environment of the Caspian Sea[163] sets forth similar arrangements. One of the functions of the Secretariat of the Caspian Sea Convention, which is based in Tehran, is to prepare and transmit to the Contracting Parties notifications, reports, and other information received. The ICPDR and the Caspian Sea Secretariat have both been notified of a number of Bank-financed projects that may affect the Danube River[164] and the Caspian Sea, respectively.[165]

An interesting question arises when not all the riparians to the shared watercourses are parties to the treaty establishing a RBO and entrusting the organization with handling notification on behalf of the riparians. How would the notification to the riparians that are not party to the treaty be handled? Should the notification in this kind of situation be sent to the organization and the states that are not parties to the organization, or should it be sent to each of the riparians separately? A case in point is the Joint Committee which is part of the Mekong River Commission established under the 1995 Agreement on the Cooperation for the Sustainable Development of the Mekong River Basin (the Mekong Agreement).[166] The Mekong Agreement includes detailed provisions on notification.[167] Of the six Mekong River riparians, only Cambodia, Lao PDR, Thailand, and Vietnam are parties to the Agreement. China and Myanmar are not parties to the Agreement, although they have been called "dialogue partners."[168] The question that arose in this and other similar situations is to whom should the notification be sent? The answer would depend on the situation of each project. If the borrower is one of the parties to the agreement

Slovenia and Ukraine, as well as the European Community), and came into force on 22 October 1998. For more on the Danube Convention *see* http://www.icpdr.org/.

163 The Caspian Sea is bounded by Azerbaijan, Iran, Kazakhstan, the Russian Federation, and Turkmenistan. The Convention was concluded in Tehran, Iran, on 4 November 2003. It entered into force on 12 August 2006. The Convention is available at: http://www.tehran-convention.org.

164 The International Commission for the Protection of the Danube River (ICPDR) was notified of a number of Bank-financed projects, including Romania (Municipal Services Project, P088252, 2006) and Bulgaria (Municipal Infrastructure Development Project, P099895, 2009).

165 The Caspian Sea Secretariat has been notified of a number of Bank financed projects, including one in Azerbaijan (Rural Investment Project, P076234, 2004).

166 The Mekong River Commission (MRC) was established under Article 11 of the Agreement, *supra* note 59, and consists of the Council, the Joint Committee, and the Secretariat.

167 *See id.*

168 For more information on the Mekong, *see* G. Browder & L. Ortolano, *'The Evolution of an International Water Resources Management Regime in the Mekong River Basin'*, 40:3 Natural Resources Journal (2000) 400–531; R. Kinna & A. Rieu-Clarke, *'The Governance Regime of the Mekong River Basin: Can the Global Water Conventions Strengthen the 1995 Mekong Agreement?'*, 2:1 International Water Law (2017).

or treaty, then under the agreement, notification would be sent to the river basin organization and each of the other non-members of the organization. The Bank would follow a similar approach if it is undertaking the notification on behalf of the borrower under the same situation.[169] If the borrower is not a member of the organization, then notification would be sent only to each of the other riparians, because the borrower is not a party to the agreement, and thus would not use the organization.

The Bank faced other unusual situations with regards to notification. The 1995 Convention for the Protection of the Marine Environment and the Coastal Region of the Mediterranean (also known as the Barcelona Convention) has the interesting feature of designating an organization not established by the Convention as responsible for some secretarial functions. Article 17 of the Convention designates UNEP to carry out those functions, which include handling of notification.[170]

In these and similar cases, notification is sent (whether by the borrower or the Bank) to the organization specified in the respective agreement. That agreement and the organization's internal rules would determine whether the organization can make the decision on the notification itself, or it needs to refer the matter to the member countries. As we have seen, the Administrative Commission, which was established by Uruguay and Argentina under the 1973 Treaty and the 1975 Statute, has the authority to determine on a preliminary basis, and within a maximum period of 30 days, whether the plan might cause significant damage to the navigational interests of the other party or the regime of the river.

In some projects the Bank went the extra step and notified both the river basin organization as well as the riparian states, although notifying one or the other would have met the policy requirement. The Odra River Basin Flood Protection Project in Poland involved the construction of a polder

---

169 In the Nam Theun 2 Power Project (NT2) (P076445, 2005), the Government of Lao PDR notified each of the other five riparians of the Mekong River, as well as the MRC, of the Project. Since the members of the MRC were themselves notified, the notification to the MRC took the form of information, rather than actual notification. For more details on the project, *see* R. Paisley et al, *'Transboundary Waters, Infrastructure Development, and Public Private Partnership: Through the Prism of the Nam Theun 2 and Xayaburi Hydropower Projects'*, 2:4 International Water Law (2017).

170 Convention for the Protection of the Marine Environment and the Coastal Region of the Mediterranean, as amended 10 June 1995; entered into force 9 July 2004. Article 17 of the Convention states: "The Contracting Parties designate the United Nations Environment Programme as responsible for carrying out the following secretarial functions … (ii) To submit to the Contracting Parties notifications, reports and other information received in accordance with articles 3, 9 and 26."

and embankment across the Odra River.[171] The River originates in the Czech Republic, flows through Poland, and then forms the border between Poland and Germany before emptying into the Baltic Sea. The three parties established the International Commission for the Protection of the Odra/Oder against Pollution (ICPOAP) in 1996.[172] The Bank, at the request of Poland, notified the ICPOAP, as well as Germany and the Czech Republic. Although both Germany and the Czech Republic responded positively, the latter advised the Bank to deal also with the ICPOAP directly.

The Nile Basin Initiative (NBI) Secretariat started to undertake notification of other Nile riparians for Bank-financed projects soon after its establishment in 1999. The Bank has agreed to the request of the Nile riparian states that the NBI Secretariat can undertake the notification to the other Nile riparian states for Bank-financed projects, following a request to this effect from the Nile Council of Ministers. The Bank agreed to this arrangement although the instrument establishing the NBI does not explicitly extend to the Secretariat the task of handling notification on behalf of the Nile riparians.[173] Under this arrangement, the NBI Secretariat acts on behalf of the borrower. It sends the notification to all the other riparians and asks for any responses they may have. It coordinates its actions during the notification process with the borrower, as well as the Bank.[174]

171 *See* Poland, Odra River Basin Flood Protection Project (P086768, 2007). The river is also known as the Oder River.

172 The Agreement was concluded by Poland, the Czech Republic, Germany, and the European Union on 1 April 1996 in Wrocław, Poland, and entered into force on 28 April 1999. For more details on the Odra/Oder River and the Agreement, *see* A. Dubicki & A. Nalberczynski, *'Development of the International Cooperation in the Oder River Basin'*, in M. Landsberg-Uczciwek, M. Adriaanse & R. Enderlein (eds.), *Management of Transboundary Waters in Europe* (Poland, 1998), at 177.

173 The Nile Basin Initiative (NBI) was established on 22 February 1999 in Dar-es-Salam, Tanzania. On that day, the Ministers of Water Resources of nine Nile riparian countries signed the minutes establishing the NBI. Thus, the NBI was not established through a treaty that was signed and ratified. For more information on the NBI, *see* www.nilebasin.org.

174 In the Eastern Nile Watershed Management Project (P111330, 2009), the NBI Secretariat notified, on behalf of Egypt and Sudan, the other Nile Basin riparian countries (Burundi, the Democratic Republic of Congo, Eritrea, Ethiopia, Kenya, Rwanda, Tanzania, and Uganda). Similarly, the NBI undertook the notification for the Egypt, West Delta Water Conservation and Irrigation Rehabilitation Project (P087970, 2007), as well as the Ethiopia, Irrigation and Drainage Project (P092353, 2007). In the latter two projects, all the other nine riparians were notified of the project by the NBI Secretariat. South Sudan joined the NBI after it seceded from the Sudan in 2011 and became the eleventh Nile riparian in 2012; *see* S. M. A. Salman, *'The New State of South Sudan and the Hydro-politics of the Nile Basin'*, 36:2 Water International (2011) 154–166.

The Bank agreed to this arrangement because it was felt that it would advance the process of the exchange of data and information and streamline the notification process among the Nile riparian states. It would also assist in strengthening the NBI Secretariat and enhancing the cooperative arrangements between the Nile states. Indeed, this approach could assist in achieving the Bank's objective of supporting the riparians' collaborative efforts to manage, share, and protect the shared watercourse, as well as the objective of dispute avoidance, which comprise a major component of the Bank policy for projects on international waterways.

It should be added that these arrangements paved the way for Ethiopia, Egypt, and Sudan to agree to handle notification for the Grand Ethiopian Renaissance Dam (GERD), which Ethiopia is currently constructing on the Blue Nile,[175] through a panel known as the 'International Panel of Experts.' The Panel consisted of two members from each of the three countries, in addition to four members from outside the Nile Basin countries. Ethiopia furnished the Panel with the necessary documents and studies on the GERD. The Panel issued its report, which endorsed the project, but recommended the carrying out of two in-depth studies. In essence, the Panel served as a mechanism for both notification by Ethiopia to Sudan and Egypt of the GERD, and dispute resolution by suggesting ways for addressing the concerns of Sudan and Egypt over the GERD following notification.[176]

---

175 Construction of the GERD commenced in April 2011. The GERD is a large dam, with a height of 145 m, and storage capacity of 74 BCM. The reservoir is more than twice the size of Lake Tana, which holds 32 BCM. The installed capacity of the GERD is 6,000 MW, with 16 turbines, each expected to generate 375 MW. This is almost three times the electricity being generated by the Aswan High Dam of 2,100 MW. The current estimates of the cost of the GERD are US$4.8 billion. Ethiopia announced from the start that it intends to finance the GERD from its own resources, with no external borrowing. For more details on the GERD, *see* S. M. A. Salman, *'The Grand Ethiopian Renaissance Dam: The Road to the Declaration of Principles and the Khartoum Document'*, 41:4 Water International (2016) 512–527, at 512. *See* also Z. Yihdego, A. Rieu-Clarke & A. Elisa Cascao (eds.) *The Grand Ethiopian Renaissance Dam and the Nile Basin – Implications for Transboundary Water Cooperation* (Routledge, London, 2018).

176 International Panel of Experts, *Grand Ethiopian Renaissance Dam: Final Report* (Addis Ababa, 31 May 2013), available at: https://www.internationalrivers.org/sites/default/files/attached-files/international_panel_of_experts_for_ethiopian_renaissance_dam-_final_report_1.pdf.
It should be added, however, that notification through the International Panel of Experts for the GERD was confined to Sudan and Egypt only, and did not include the Nile other riparians. This was a marked departure from notification through the Nile Basin Initiative (NBI) Secretariat which included all the Nile riparians for any project on the Nile, as discussed earlier.

Thus, the Bank has been honouring and following the riparians' agreed upon agreements and arrangements, and notification was undertaken following procedures set forth therein. In fact, the Bank went a step further and agreed to the request of the Nile Basin Ministers of Water Resources that the NBI would undertake notification for Bank-financed projects on the Nile, although the Minutes establishing the NBI do not grant the NBI such explicit authority.

5.8 *Other Possible Mechanisms for Notification*

In addition to the prospective borrower, the Bank, and the institutional arrangements agreed upon by the riparians, notification for Bank-financed projects has been undertaken in some exceptional cases, through a third party, mostly United Nations agencies.

Territories under the administration of the United Nations presented special challenges with regard to notification. One such example was Kosovo while it was being administered by the United Nations Mission in Kosovo (UNMIK). The Bank decided that for Bank-financed projects, the UNMIK would be approached and asked to undertake the notification on behalf of Kosovo. If UNMIK indicated to the Bank that it did not wish to do so, the Bank would undertake the notification provided UNMIK had no objection to the Bank doing so. However, UNMIK agreed to undertake the notification on behalf of Kosovo.[177]

Undertaking notification through UNMIK was based on an earlier precedent where a similar United Nations administration was used. That was the case with the Lesotho Highlands Water Project, which presented some challenges as to whom to notify, and by whom. This multipurpose project involved the construction of dams and tunnels and the development and transfer of water resources from the highlands region of Lesotho to the Republic of South Africa for municipal and industrial use.[178] The water to be exported to South Africa is from the Sengue River,[179] which originates in Lesotho.[180]

---

177 One project that involved this arrangement was the Kosovo, Private Sector Participation in Water Supply and Sanitation in Gjakovë-Rahovec (P072913, 2002), which involved use of the water of the Drin/Drim River that Kosovo shares with Albania. UNMIK agreed to send the notification about the project to Albania, to which Albania responded positively.

178 Lesotho, Highlands Water Project – Phase 1A (P001409, 1998). Phase 1A involved construction of the Kaste Dam on the Sengue River, a transfer tunnel, delivery tunnel, and an underground power station. Phase 1B included the construction of the Mohale Dam on the Sengue River, as well as a tunnel and other diversions.

179 The Sengue River is also known as the Senqu River.

180 The basis of the Lesotho, Highlands Water Project – Phase 1A (P001396, 1991) is the Treaty on the Lesotho Highlands Water Project between the Government of the Kingdom of Lesotho and the Government of the Republic of South Africa, Maseru, 24 October 1986.

The River becomes the Orange River upon entry into South Africa, and thereafter forms the boundary between South Africa and Namibia before emptying into the Atlantic Ocean. The riparian states of the River are therefore Lesotho, South Africa, and Namibia.

The issue of notification came up in the mid-1980s while Namibia was still under the administration of the United Nations Council for South West Africa (Namibia) (UN Council). The UN Council was established under a UN General Assembly resolution in 1967.[181] Two intricate questions arose (i) who should undertake the notification: Lesotho or South Africa? and (ii) who should be notified? With regards to question (i), the issue also arose as to whether notification should be undertaken by South Africa, the beneficiary of the Project, or by Lesotho, where the Project is located. The question was resolved by a request to the Bank from both countries to undertake the notification on their behalf. On question (ii), it was decided that the Bank would send the notification to the UN Council which was then the legal administering authority for Namibia. This was done in November 1984, and the UN Council voiced no objection to the Project in April 1985.[182] The World Bank also asked Lesotho to consult with the South West Africa People's Organization (SWAPO), which was recognized as the representative of the people of Namibia. SWAPO also had no objection to the Project.

However, the Project was not presented to the Bank Executive Directors by the time Namibia gained its independence on 21 March 1990. For that reason, the Bank decided to seek a reconfirmation from the newly constituted Namibian government of the no-objection received from the UN Council and from SWAPO. Accordingly, a new notification was sent to the Namibian government in May 1990, updating the earlier notification letter and project details submitted to it, and Namibia voiced no objection to the Project.

Challenging situations are faced when there is no central government with effective legal authority in a country to notify. In such cases, the Bank has notified the Executive Director representing such a country in the Bank Board.[183]

The Treaty laid down detailed provisions on the Project, including the payment of royalties to Lesotho by South Africa. Project preparation commenced thereafter, and the Project was approved by the Bank in 1991. *See* FAO, *supra* note 53, at 172; *see also:* http://www.fao.org/docrep/W7414B/w7414b0w.htm.

181 UNGA, *Question of South West Africa*, UN. Doc. A/RES/2248 (S-V), 19 May 1967.

182 In making the decision, the UN Council consulted with the UN Office of the Legal Affairs and made it clear that this was without prejudice to the rights of the sovereign state of Namibia upon its independence. That was the reason the Bank decided to notify the Namibian government once it was established.

183 This is the practice that the Bank has followed with regards to Somalia since the early 1990s.

As such, in addition to notification being undertaken by the borrower and the Bank, other interesting approaches have been evolving within the Bank. These approaches have recognized and utilized existing arrangements and agreements and have addressed new challenging situations with innovative legal methodologies; thus, continuing to enrich Bank practice and precedents in this field.

5.9 *Exceptions to the Notification Requirement*

As specified earlier, the Policy requires, as a general rule, notification of all the riparians of a project on an international waterway. However, the Policy provides for three exceptions to the Bank's requirement that the other riparian states be notified of the proposed project. These exceptions are:

(a) For any ongoing schemes, projects involving additions or alterations that require rehabilitation, construction, or other changes that in the judgment of the Bank (i) will not adversely change the quality or quantity of water flows to the other riparians; and (ii) will not be adversely affected by the other riparians' possible water use.[184]

(b) Water resource surveys and feasibility studies on or involving international waterways. However, the state proposing such activities includes in the terms of reference for the activities an examination of any potential riparian issues.

(c) Any project that relates to a tributary of an international waterway where the tributary runs exclusively in one state, and the state is the lowest downstream riparian, unless there is concern that the project could cause appreciable harm to other states.

The first exception has been consistently interpreted to apply to rehabilitation of existing schemes. It is worth noting that although the Policy has not established a threshold for notification, it has set such a threshold for application to this exception. The works to be financed for the rehabilitation of the existing schemes should be minor and should not adversely change the quality or quantity of water flow to other riparians. If there is doubt about this determination, then the Policy requires notifying the Executive Director or Directors

---

184 According to the Policy, this exception applies only to minor additions or alterations to the ongoing scheme; it does not cover works and activities that would exceed the original scheme, change its nature, or so alter or expand its scope and extent as to make it appear a new or different scheme. In case of doubt regarding the extent to which a project meets the criteria of this exception, the Executive Directors representing the riparians concerned are informed and given at least two months to reply. Even if projects meet the criteria of this exception, the Bank tries to secure compliance with the requirements of any agreement or arrangement between the riparians.

representing the affected riparian states, providing them with the project details, and giving them at least two months to reply.

It seems that this exception was crafted as a compromise to the Bank staff who demanded a threshold for notification rather than making notification a rule for every project on shared watercourses, regardless of its effects on other riparians. However, the exception begs the very same question it attempts to answer: If notification is not required for projects for rehabilitation of existing schemes where the project will not adversely change the quality or quantity of water flows to the other riparians, and will not be adversely affected by the other riparians' possible water use, then why should notification be required for other projects with the same *di minimis* effects on the shared watercourse? As a result, the exception has created a window for the Bank staff, as well as riparians who are concerned about notification, to design their projects around this exception to avoid notification.

The second exception, dealing with water resources surveys and feasibility studies, should be distinguished from detailed design and engineering studies. The latter indicates an advanced stage in project preparation and requires notifying other states, which is not the case with surveys and feasibility studies.

The third exception relates to a tributary of a shared watercourse originating and running exclusively in the lowest downstream riparian. Unlike the two exceptions discussed above, this exception was not included in the original 1985 OMS. It was added to the policy in 1994, following discussion of a project in Burma (currently Myanmar).[185] The project consisted of the construction of an earth dam about 110 feet high on the Yin River and diversion structures about 17 miles downstream of the dam. The Yin River originates within Burma and joins the Irrawaddy River there. The Irrawaddy River is the largest river in Burma. It is fed by two tributaries, the Daying and the Jiang, both originating within China, with the latter tributary fed by a sub-tributary originating within India. Burma is the lowest downstream riparian of the Irrawaddy River, and from Burma, the River empties into the Indian Ocean.[186]

The international waterway aspect of the project centred on the facts that the project is on a tributary originating within the lowest downstream riparian and joining an international waterway, the Irrawaddy River, there. Although fed by some tributaries originating in China and India, the Irrawaddy River itself runs largely in Burma. It was argued strongly that the project would not cause appreciable harm to the other riparians, nor would it be appreciably

185 *See* Burma, Second Tank Irrigation Project (1988).

186 The name of the country was changed from Burma to Myanmar in 1989. More than 90 percent of the catchment area of the Irrawaddy River is in Myanmar.

harmed by the other riparians' possible use of water. According to this argument, the Yin River runs only in Burma, the lowest downstream riparian. Based on this argument, a decision was taken that since there was no conceivable harm, there was no issue,[187] and, accordingly, notification of other riparians was not required.

Subsequently, a third exception was added and included in the 1994 version of the Bank policy as paragraph 7(c). This exception seems to have been influenced by the fact that the Irrawaddy River is largely a Burmese river, with only a small portion of the catchment area and the basin falling outside of Burma. However, the exception overlooked some basic legal facts.

First, this exception runs contrary to the established and accepted definition of the term international watercourse. It should be recalled in this regard that the Permanent Court of International Justice in the *Oder River* case determined that the jurisdiction of the International Commission for the Oder River extended to tributaries of such river.[188] After discussing the principle of community of interest of riparian states, the Court concluded: "This community of interest in a navigable river becomes the basis of a common legal right, the essential features of which are the perfect equality of all riparian States in the use of the whole of the course of the river and the exclusion of any preferential privileges of any one riparian State in relation to the others."[189] Along these lines, the UN Watercourses Convention defines the term 'international watercourse' to mean "a watercourse, parts of which are situated in different

187 Although the approach of 'no conceivable harm, no issue' has no basis in OMS 2.32 of 1985, it prevailed in this particular project.

188 *See Case Relating to the Territorial Jurisdiction of the International Commission of the River Oder*, 1929 P.C.I.J. (ser. A) No. 16 (*Great Britain, Czechoslovak Republic, Denmark, France, Germany and Sweden v. Poland*). The issue before the Permanent Court of International Justice was whether the jurisdiction of the International Commission of the Oder River extended, under the provisions of the Treaty of Versailles, to sections of the tributaries of the Oder, namely the Warthe and Netze, which are situated in Poland. Whereas Poland maintained that the jurisdiction of the Oder Commission excluded sections of those tributaries within Polish territory, the other six countries felt that the navigable portions of those tributaries should not be excluded from the Commission's jurisdiction. The Court ruled that the jurisdiction of the Commission extended to certain tributaries of the Oder River situated within Poland.

189 The reference by the Permanent Court of International Justice to "international fluvial law in general" led many scholars to conclude that the notion of "the equality of all riparians" enunciated by the Court goes beyond navigation and applies equally to non-navigation. *See* J. Lipper, *'Equitable Utilization'*, in A. H. Garretson et al (eds.), *The Law of International Drainage Basins* (London: Oceana Publications, 1967), at 22–23.

States."[190] Thus, the Yin River is indeed a part and parcel of international watercourse.

Second, as discussed above, the definition of the term 'international waterway' under the Bank policy includes tributaries of such a waterway.[191] Thus, the exception does not comport with the Bank Policy itself. Moreover, the exception failed to treat the Irrawaddy River and its tributaries as one basin where cooperation and goodwill of all the riparians is required for its efficient utilization, as mandated by the Bank Policy.

Third, the exception failed to take into account the fact that the project would assist Burma in establishing rights to the waters of the Yin River, and that such water rights would be claimed as established or acquired rights in any future negotiations with the other riparians over the entire Irrawady River. The waters that Burma would claim as established rights would not be available for the future uses of the other riparians of the Irrawaddy Basin. This concept of foreclosure of future uses has been discussed above.[192] Thus, the exception runs contrary to the concept of foreclosure of future uses that the Bank Policy has helped clarify and elaborate.

It is worth noting that this exception to the notification requirement used the term 'appreciable harm' in line with the rest of the Policy, but unlike the first exception discussed above, which used the term 'adverse effect'. In this way, the two exceptions under the same paragraph of the Policy have used two different terminologies for the threshold for the activities financed to fall under said exception.

Another observation about this exception is the use of the term 'downstream.' The terms 'downstream' and 'upstream' riparians have not been used in any of the Bank policies for projects on international watercourses. However, it seems that in this particular exception there was a clear need to use the term 'downstream riparian' as the exception is referring to a specific riparian on a specific location on the shared river; an unfortunate necessity emanating from an unnecessary exception.

Thus, to circumvent its strict requirement of notification of all the riparians of Bank-financed projects on international waterways, the Bank Policy created three exceptions to the notification requirement. However, these exceptions

190 UN Watercourses Convention, *supra* note 62, art. 2(b).

191 *See* paragraph 1(b) of OP 7.50, *supra* note 141, which defines international waterway to mean "(a) any river, canal, lake, or similar body of water that forms a boundary between, or any river or body of surface water that flows through, two or more states, whether Bank members or not; (b) any tributary or other body of surface water that is a component of any waterway described in (a) above."

192 *See supra* note 18.

themselves raise more questions than they answer. Indeed, the last exception does not comport with the Bank Policy itself, or to international water law. However, those three exceptions would not be needed if the Policy were to be amended to include a threshold for notification – significant adverse effect or appreciable harm. Those exceptions would then be subsumed under the threshold of significant adverse effect or appreciable harm to establish the new basis for notification.

Despite the issues raised by these three exceptions, as well as by the inclusion of semi-enclosed coastal waters in the definition of waterways, the World Bank Policy issued in 1985 enriched the already extensive practice and experience that the Bank had accumulated since it started financing projects on international waterways in the late 1940s and early 1950s, particularly with regards to notification. The 1985 Policy underwent some minor amendments and was reissued in 2001, and again in 2012 as OP/BP 7.50.[193] As stated above, the 2012 versions are still in force and effect. The richness of the practice of the Bank is also evident in the responses to notification, including how to handle objections, as will be discussed in the next two parts of this monograph.

Part 6: Possible Responses by the Notified States

The UN Watercourses Convention and the Bank Policy for Projects on International Waterways both identify the possible responses by the notified state or states to the notification for planned measures or projects submitted to them by the notifying state, or through indirect procedures. The Convention lists the possible responses as (i) absence of reply within the period specified for the response; (ii) request for additional time to study the documents concerning the planned measure; (iii) request for additional information; and (iv) communication that the planned measure would be inconsistent with the provisions of Articles 5 or 7 of the Convention (on reasonable and equitable utilization and the obligation not to cause significant harm, respectively).

Similarly, the Bank Policy specifies the possible responses as (i) a positive response from the notified state or states in the form of consent, no objection, support for the project, or confirmation that the project will not harm their interest; (ii) absence of response within the period specified for response; and (iii) objection to the project. Thus, the Bank, unlike the Watercourses Convention, was not shy in using the term "objection."

193 *See supra* note 141.

However, Bank practical experience has shown that the list of possible responses for notification is actually wider than those specified by the Watercourses Convention and the Bank Policy, and can include at least seven possibilities. Each of these possible responses under the Watercourses Convention and the Bank Policy and practice are described in turn.

6.1 *Request for Additional Time*

One or more of the notified riparian states may ask for more time to study and evaluate the project details furnished to them with the notification letter. Although the Bank Policy itself does not provide for this kind of situation in the Policy, the Bank has, in practice, and as indicated in its Good Practice, always agreed to extend the period established for the response, and has set a new date, mostly corresponding with the new time frame requested by the riparian. As discussed in part 3 of this monograph, the UN Watercourses Convention provides for such a possibility, and recommends that a period equal to the initial period of six months be given to the notified states.[194]

6.2 *Request for Additional Information*

The UN Watercourses Convention provides explicitly for a request for additional information, but qualifies the duty of the notifying state by stating that such a state is not obliged to provide data or information vital to its national defence or security.[195] Nevertheless, that state shall cooperate in good faith with the other watercourse states with a view to providing as much information as possible under the circumstances.

Although the Bank Policy does not provide for this kind of situation in the Policy itself, it has included such a possibility in the Good Practice,[196] and the actual practice of the Bank has shown a wide range of requests for additional information which the Bank has acceded to, or has asked the notifying state to accede to. As examples, the notified riparians may claim that the project details furnished to them are not adequate to enable them to make a determination

194 UN Watercourse Convention, *supra* note 62, art. 13.

195 As discussed above, Article 31 of the UN Watercourses Convention, *id.*, states: "Nothing in the present Convention obliges a watercourse State to provide data or information vital to its national defense or security. Nevertheless, that State shall cooperate in good faith with the other watercourse States with a view to providing as much information as possible under the circumstances."

196 Paragraph 4 of the GP 7.50, *supra* note 140, stated: "Upon being notified that a riparian may seek additional information or clarification, staff should make every effort to provide it and allow a reasonable period for study and response." As indicated above, the Good Practice memoranda have been discontinued.

on the effects of the project. Accordingly, they may ask for additional information shortly after they have received the notification letter, and within the period specified for reply.

The additional information requested in many instances may relate to the quantitative effects of the project. There may be requests for the environmental impact assessment of the project which might not have been ready by the time the notification was sent to the other riparians, or for clarifications of some issues raised by the EIA. The request could also relate to clarification regarding the exact location of the project, including a request for a detailed map, if such a map was not included in the original notification. Some notified states have also requested more specificity on the amount of water to be abstracted for small-scale irrigation and water supply sub-projects in demand driven and social funds projects.[197]

In a few instances, the request has gone beyond the project, and asked for more information on earlier projects that the Bank has financed in the same country or on the same waterway. As such, the notified riparian is seeking information on the cumulative effects of Bank-financed projects on the shared watercourse. As an international cooperative financial institution, the Bank would need to do its best to provide such information to the riparian or riparians that requested it. The request for additional information underscores the need to furnish adequate project details in the first instance so as to avoid the delays that this kind of request could result in.

One question that has arisen in connection with requests for additional information concerns the refusal of the notifying state to furnish the additional information requested by the notified state. Can the Bank provide such information to the notified state even if the notification was undertaken by the borrowing riparian state? As a first step, the Bank would discuss the matter with the notifying state, and ascertain the reasons for its reluctance to provide the information itself. The Bank would try to persuade that state to furnish the requested information if it found the request for such information is reasonable and warranted. If the state persists in its refusal, the Bank could offer to furnish such information on its behalf. If the state objects to the Bank furnishing such requested information, and the Bank has determined that the need for such information is reasonable, then the Bank would extend application of paragraph 4 of the OP 7.50 which requires the Bank to discontinue processing of the project if the borrower objects to giving notification and objects to the Bank doing so. Anticipating this situation, the Watercourses Convention

197 This request was made by Egypt and Sudan in connection with the Ethiopia, Social Rehabilitation and Development Fund Project (P000771, 1996).

obliges the notifying state to cooperate with the notified States by providing them, on request, with any additional data and information that is available and necessary for an accurate evaluation.

6.3 *Request for Additional Information and Time*

In this case the request from the notified riparian or riparians would combine both (6.1) and (6.2) above. The notified riparian would state that it needs additional information and additional time to evaluate this information. The request could be sent immediately after the notification letter was sent. It could also be sent towards the end of the period provided for sending a response.[198] This situation is provided for in GP 7.50, which recommended providing both the requested information and the additional time needed to evaluate it. Requests for both additional information and time is more common than for either time or information alone.

Requests for additional information and additional time received by the Bank from the notified state after the date set for response in the notification letter are dealt with on a case-by-case basis, depending on the timing and type of information requested.[199] If the request is received a few days after the date set for response, and the information requested may be relevant to decision-making, and there is still time for presentation of the project to the Executive Directors, then the Bank would provide the requested information and set a new date for response. However, if the request is received some time after the date set for response, or the information requested is not that important to making the decision, then the Bank would send the information, reconfirm that the project would not cause appreciable harm, and explain that it would proceed with project processing as planned.[200] The Bank would also encourage the borrower, if it has undertaken the notification itself, to follow those same procedures. If the request for information is received after the project was approved by the Executive Directors, then the information would be provided and the new situation would be explained in the reply to preclude further requests for more information, questions, or challenges.

198 *See* Bulgaria, Municipal Infrastructure Development Project (P099895, 2009).

199 GP 7.50, *supra* note 140, para. 4.

200 Those decisions would be made by senior management of the Bank on the recommendation of the task team for the project, following the same procedures provided for under paragraph 4 of BP 7.50, *supra* note 141.

6.4 *No Response*

Both the Watercourses Convention and the Bank Policy address the issue of no response to a notification. The Convention states that if, within the period specified for reply the notifying state receives no communication, it may, subject to its obligations under Articles 5 and 7 (equitable and reasonable utilization and the obligation against causing harm), proceed with the implementation of the planned measures, in accordance with the notification and any other data and information provided to the notified states. Article 16 of the Convention goes on to state that any claim to compensation by a notified state that has failed to reply within the specified period may be offset by the costs incurred by the notifying state for action undertaken after the expiration of the time for a reply which would not have been undertaken if the notified state had objected within that period.

The absence of response from the notified states has been a main feature of the notification process for Bank projects. Some states do not want to give explicit consent or objection to the project, so they simply do not respond. The question that has arisen within the Bank is whether failure to respond should be construed as a no-objection to the project. The Bank has taken that position based on the determination that the projects it finances do not cause appreciable harm to other riparian states. Failure of the notified state to challenge that determination, when they have been given ample opportunity and information to do so, is taken by the Bank as an implicit confirmation to its determination that the project will indeed not cause appreciable harm to the notified states. The Bank has usually described this situation as "absence of unfavourable response."

6.5 *Positive Response or No-Objection*

It is worth noting that the UN Watercourses Convention does not explicitly address the possibility of a positive response. The Convention only indicates that the notified states would communicate their findings to the notifying state as early as possible within the specified period. It goes on to address the situation where the notified state finds the implementation of the planned measure to be inconsistent with Articles 5 or 7 of the Convention (equitable and reasonable utilization and the obligation not to cause harm, respectively).[201]

Under the Bank Policy and practice, the positive response from some or all the riparians could take one of different forms. It could be a consent, or even enthusiastic support for the project; it could be a confirmation of the

201 UN Watercourses Convention, *supra* note 62, art. 17.

determination made in the notification letter that the project will not harm their interests; or it could simply be a general no-objection to the project.

Despite the difficulties surrounding international waterways by reason of the competing demands of the different riparians, there have been a good number of cases where riparians have provided some form of no-objection to Bank-financed projects. This positive response is usually facilitated by the confirmation by the Bank, when it sends the notification, that the project will not cause appreciable harm to any of the riparians; a determination that should obviously be supported by the data and information laid out in the project details. The positive response can also be received from the river basin organization on behalf of the riparian states when the notification was sent to such organization.

6.6 *Qualified No-Objection*

There have been instances where the borrower or the Bank has received a qualified no-objection from one of the notified riparian states. Such a response would indicate that the state concerned has no-objection to the project provided that certain actions are taken with regards to the project under consideration. In one project involving the abstraction of water from a shared aquifer, the notified state gave its no-objection to the project provided that no drilling of wells would take place within a certain distance of the borders of each of the two countries.[202] This was accepted by both the Bank and the borrower because of the reciprocal nature of the condition.

In another project, one of the notified states gave its no-objection to the project provided that the Bank and the borrower would supply that state regularly during the project period with reports on the implementation of the environment management plan for the project and the actual effects of the project on that riparian.[203] In its rejection of this condition, the Bank reiterated its determination that the project would not cause appreciable harm to the other riparians, and clarified that periodic reports are usually issued for all Bank-financed projects which can be accessed and reviewed by any interested party.[204]

There may be situations where it may not be easy to distinguish between requests for additional information and the case of a qualified no-objection. This determination would depend on the wording of the response received from

---

202 *See* Jordan, Disi-Amman Water Conveyor Project, *supra* note 147.

203 *See* Nepal, Power Development Project (P043311, 2003).

204 The World Bank Project Status web page includes information on each operation funded by the Bank, available at http://projects.worldbank.org.

such a notified state. The notified state may ask for a cumulative impact assessment of all Bank-financed projects on that specific waterway, to ascertain the effects of all these projects, and not just that particular project. This could be a request for additional information of such a cumulative impact statement. It could also be a condition for its no-objection. In one such case the Bank reconfirmed the *de minimis* effects of the project at hand, and clarified that a cumulative impact assessment was beyond the scope of that project, but could be done as part of the EIA in one future project. Thus, the Bank classified the request as one for additional information that was not available, rather than a qualified no-objection.[205]

However, there may be cases where the qualification to the no-objection is more in the nature of a conditional no-objection, than a qualified no-objection. Such a determination would be arrived at depending on the nature of the response. For example, if the notified state questioned the height of the dam to be constructed under the project, or the design of that dam, and asked for decreasing the height or changing the design, then this would most likely be classified as a conditional no-objection. Under such a situation, the Bank and the borrower would provide clarifications to the notified state as to why the project should be kept as proposed. If the notified state insists on its condition, then this conditional no-objection would be treated as an objection, and be dealt with under the procedures set forth in the next part of this monograph.

6.7 *Objection by One or More of the Riparian States*

As indicated above, the Watercourses Convention does not use the term "objection." Rather the Convention refers to objection in these words: "If a notified State finds that implementation of the planned measures would be inconsistent with the provisions of articles 5 or 7, it shall attach to its finding a documented explanation setting forth the reasons for the finding."[206] Perhaps the drafters of the Convention might have thought and decided that the word "objection" is too strong a term to use in an instrument intended to be a framework for cooperation. Nonetheless, this type of response can, and indeed should, be classified as an objection.

205 The Ethiopia Urban Water Supply and Sanitation Project (P101473, 2007) involved abstraction of water from the Omo River, which flows into Lake Turkana. The Lake is shared by Ethiopia and Kenya, with the largest part of the Lake falling within Kenya. Kenya asked for more information on the service level and net abstraction, as well as the effects of other projects on the Omo River. The Bank confirmed the minimal effects of the project, and indicated that it would make the EIA available once it was completed.

206 UN Watercourses Convention, *supra* note 62, arts. 15 and 17.

Although the notification letter and the project details in Bank-financed projects usually confirm that the project will not cause appreciable harm to any of the riparians, or will not affect the quantity or quality of the waters of the shared waterway,[207] both the determination and confirmation have been challenged by some riparians in some projects, as we have seen in the previous parts of this monograph. The examples of the Ghab Project in Syria and the objection of Turkey, and the Igdir-Aksu Project in Turkey and the objection of Iran, were discussed and elaborated on above. A detailed discussion of the issue of objection by some riparians under the Watercourses Convention and the Bank Policy and practice, and how such an objection is dealt with, are given in the next part of this monograph.

Part 7: Procedures in Case of Objection Following Notification

As discussed in the previous part of this monograph, one possible response to the notification for planned measures from one or more of the notified riparians could be an objection to the project. The Watercourses Convention, as mentioned before, has shied away from the term "objection", perhaps as being too strong a term for a treaty aiming at cooperation among the different riparians. Instead, the Convention states: "If a notified State finds that implementation of the planned measures would be inconsistent with the provisions of articles 5 or 7."[208] On the other hand, the Bank Policy has explicitly used the term "objection" by stating "If the other riparians object to the proposed project."[209]

The objection from the notified state or states could be for appropriate legitimate reasons related to the likely negative effects of the proposed project on the notified state or states, or on the shared watercourse itself. However, the objection may be for reasons not related to the proposed project itself, such as the poor diplomatic relations between the notifying and the objecting states, or to some other disputes between these states. Regardless of the causes for the objection, there is the requirement to respond to it. The procedures set forth by the different legal instruments, the Watercourses Convention, as well as the

207 As discussed above, in the presentation of the project to its Executive Directors, the Bank needs to confirm that the project would not cause appreciable harm to other riparians. *See* OP 7.50, *supra* note 141, para. 8.

208 UN Watercourses Convention, *supra* note 62, arts. 15 and 17.

209 BP 7.50, *supra* note 141, para. 6.

World Bank Policies and practice address this matter with some slight variations, as discussed below.

7.1 *Procedures Recommended by the IIL and ILA for Dealing with Objections*

The IIL and ILA adopted provisions addressing the issue of how to deal with an objection by one of the riparian states to a proposed project. The Salzburg Resolution issued by the IIL in 1961[210] requires, in cases where an objection is made to a project on a shared watercourse, the notifying and objecting states to enter into negotiations with a view to reaching an agreement within a reasonable period of time. The Resolution recommends that those states have recourse to technical experts and, should occasion arise, to appropriate agencies in order to arrive at solutions assuring the greatest advantage to all concerned. It goes on to oblige the notifying state, in conformity with the principle of good faith, to refrain from undertaking the works or utilization which are the object of the dispute, or from taking any other measures which might aggravate the dispute, or render agreement more difficult. If the interested states fail to reach agreement within a reasonable period of time, the Resolution recommends that the parties submit to judicial settlement or arbitration the question of whether the project is contrary to the above rules.[211]

The ILA Helsinki Rules of 1966 do not deal with an objection to a proposed project *per se*, but rather with a question or dispute relating to the present or future utilization of the waters of an international drainage basin. The Rules recommend that the basin states try to resolve such a question or dispute through negotiations.[212] Failing that, they may refer the question or dispute to a joint agency, and request the agency to survey the international drainage basin and to formulate plans or recommendations for the fullest and most efficient use thereof in the interests of all such States. If the question or a dispute cannot be resolved in this manner, the Rules recommend that the parties seek the good offices, or jointly request the mediation of a qualified international organization or of a qualified person. If the parties fail to resolve their dispute through those procedures, the Rules recommend that they form a commission

---

210 *Supra* note 41.

211 *Id.*, arts. 6–8. According to Article 8 of the Resolution, if the state objecting to the works or utilization refuses to submit to judicial settlement or arbitration, the other state is free, subject to its responsibilities, to go ahead while remaining bound by its obligation arising from the provisions of Articles 2–4 (the rights of utilization by other states, equitable sharing and the right to compensation in case of losses).

212 The Helsinki Rules, *supra* note 45, devote the entire Chapter 6 for dispute prevention and dispute settlement, and Articles XXX to XXXVII of Chapter 6 deal with dispute settlement.

of inquiry, or an *ad hoc* conciliation commission, which shall endeavor to find a solution.[213] Finally, the Rules recommend submitting the dispute to an *ad hoc* arbitral tribunal or to the International Court of Justice if the commission cannot reach a solution, or the solution was not acceptable to the parties.

7.2 *Procedures for Dealing with Objections under the UN Watercourses Convention*

The procedures set forth under the UN Watercourses Convention for dealing with an objection from one or more of the notified riparian states to a planned measure are, by and large, based on the procedures set forth by the IIL and the ILA. The Watercourses Convention stipulates that if a notified state finds that implementation of the planned measures would be inconsistent with Articles 5 and 7 of the Convention (regarding equitable and reasonable utilization and the obligation not to cause significant harm, respectively), it shall attach to its finding a documented explanation setting forth the reasons for the finding.[214] Subsequently, the notifying state and the notified state shall enter into consultations and, if necessary, negotiations with a view to arriving at an equitable resolution of the situation. The consultations and negotiations shall be conducted on the basis that each state must in good faith pay reasonable regard to the rights and legitimate interests of the other state.[215] During the course of the consultations and negotiations, the notifying state shall, if so requested by the notified state at the time it makes the communication, refrain from implementing or permitting the implementation of the planned measures for a period of six months unless otherwise agreed.

The Convention goes on to state that in the event that the implementation of the planned measures is of the utmost urgency in order to protect public health, public safety or other equally important interests, the state planning the measures may, subject to Articles 5 and 7, immediately proceed with implementation. In such a case, a formal declaration of the urgency of the measures shall be communicated without delay to the other watercourse states. However, the states planning such measures shall at the request of any of the other watercourse states enter into consultations and negotiations with such a state.[216]

---

213 The Helsinki Rules, *id.*, recommend that the conciliation commission be constituted in the manner set forth in the Annex entitled "Model Rules for the Constitution of the Conciliation Commission for the Settlement of a Dispute."

214 UN Watercourses Convention, *supra* note 62, art. 15.

215 *Id.*, art. 17.

216 *Id.*, art. 19.

In addition to these special provisions dealing with consultations and negotiations concerning planned measures, the Watercourses Convention includes a separate article (Article 33) on the settlement of disputes.[217] This Article lays out a number of procedures for resolving disputes, but underscores the fact-finding process for dispute settlement.

Indeed, fact-finding is the only binding dispute settlement process under the Convention, although the parties are only urged to consider the recommendations of the fact-finding commission in good faith. Article 33 of the Convention states that in the event of a dispute between two or more parties concerning the interpretation or application of the Convention, the parties concerned shall, in the absence of an applicable agreement between them, seek a settlement of the dispute by peaceful means in accordance with the provisions set forth in that article.

The fact-finding process starts with negotiations at the request of one of the disputants. If the parties cannot reach agreement by negotiation, they may jointly seek the good offices of, or request mediation or conciliation by, a third party, or make use of any joint watercourse institutions established by them, or agree to submit the dispute to arbitration or to the International Court of Justice.

However, if after six months from the time of the request for negotiations the parties have not been able to settle their dispute through negotiations or any other means referred to above, the dispute shall be submitted, at the request of any of the parties, to impartial fact-finding. A fact-finding commission shall be established, composed of one member nominated by each party, with the third party not having the nationality of any of the parties concerned, chosen by the two nominated members, who shall serve as chairman. If the members fail to agree on a chairman within three months of the initial request, the chairman will be nominated by the Secretary-General of the United Nations, and shall not have the nationality of any of the parties to the dispute, or of any riparian state of the watercourse concerned. The three members shall constitute the fact-finding commission, which shall determine its own procedures.[218] The expenses of the Commission shall be borne equally by the parties concerned, regardless of the nature of the recommendations.

---

217 *Id.*, art. 33. In addition, the Convention includes a detailed annex on arbitration, consisting of 14 articles.

218 Article 33(5) of the Convention, *id.*, states that if one of the parties fails to nominate a member within three months of the initial request, any other party concerned may request the Secretary-General of the United Nations to appoint a person who shall not have the nationality of any of the parties to the dispute or of any riparian state of the

The parties are obliged to provide the Commission with such information as it may require and, on request, to permit the Commission to have access to their respective territory and to inspect any facilities, plant, equipment, construction, or natural feature relevant for the purpose of its inquiry. The Commission shall adopt its report by a majority vote, and shall submit that report to the parties concerned setting forth its findings and the reasons therefor, and such recommendations as it deems appropriate for an equitable solution of the dispute, which the parties shall consider in good faith.

Although the fact-finding process is the only binding dispute settlement process under the Convention, there is no obligation on the parties to abide by the recommendations of the Commission; they are only obliged to consider such recommendations in good faith. The fact-finding process under the Watercourses Convention has similarities to the opinion of independent experts' process under the World Bank policy for projects on international waterways, as will be discussed in the next section of this part of the monograph.

7.3 *Bank Procedures for Dealing with Objections*

As we have seen in the previous parts of this monograph, the objection to the Ghab Project in Syria and to the Igdir-Aksu-Eregli-Ercis Irrigation Project in Turkey both had played a significant role in the evolution of the Bank policy for projects on international waterways. Turkey's objection to the Ghab Project in Syria prompted the Bank to issue its first policy in 1956 – OM 8 – establishing an early warning system for a close, careful and cautious look at projects on international waterways. As discussed above, OM 5.05 issued in 1965 added some substantive and procedural rules to OM 8.

It took 20 years and another objection for the Bank to issue another more detailed and elaborate policy in 1985, replacing its 1965 OM. As discussed above, that objection came from Iran over a project in Turkey. Since that time a number of ambiguities and gaps regarding the notification process under the policy were filled through the implementation experience, including how to deal with the different kinds of responses, as well as objections, to a proposed Bank-financed project.

OMS 2.32 issued in 1985 has put in place detailed procedures for dealing with responses from notified riparians, including procedures to address the issue of an objection from one of the notified riparians. In addition to specific provisions in the OMS on notification, Annex A to the OMS deals with objection and

watercourse concerned (similar to the chairman of the fact-finding commission). The person so appointed shall constitute a single-member commission.

is titled "Technical Advice of Independent Experts." These procedures are now spelt out in paragraphs 6 through 12 of BP 7.50.[219]

BP 7.50 requires the Country Director (CD), in collaboration with the Legal Vice Presidency (LEGVP) and other departments concerned, to send a memorandum on the objection to the Regional Vice President, with a copy to the LEGVP. The memorandum addresses:

(a) the nature of the riparian issues;
(b) the Bank staff's assessment of the objection raised, including the reasons for such an objection, and any available supporting data;
(c) the staff's assessment of whether the proposed project will cause appreciable harm to the interests of the other riparians, or be appreciably harmed by the other riparians' possible water use;
(d) the question of whether the circumstances of the case require that the Bank, before taking any further action, urge the parties to resolve the issues through amicable means such as consultations, negotiations, and good offices[220] (which will normally be resorted to when the other riparians' objections are substantiated); and
(e) the question of whether the objections are of such a nature that it is advisable to obtain an additional opinion from independent experts.

Thus, the decision to obtain an opinion from independent experts is preceded by attempts to resolve the issues regarding the objection through consultations, negotiations, and good offices. Similarly, resort to the fact-finding commission under the UN Watercourses Convention is preceded by attempts to resolve the issues through negotiations, use of good offices, mediation or conciliation by a third party.

If a decision is taken to seek the opinion of independent experts, then a number of units within the Bank would be involved in the process of appointment, financing, and interacting with the experts. The reason behind the involvement of a number of units is to guarantee that the process is credible – that the experts would carry their responsibilities in an independent atmosphere. The issues of conflict of interest and conflict of responsibility would

219 *Id.*, paras. 6–12.

220 The approaches of negotiations and good offices under the Policy are merely suggestions to the parties and not a requirement. Paragraph 3 of the OP, *supra* note 141, states that in cases where the differences remain unresolved between the beneficiary state and the other riparians prior to financing the project, the Bank normally urges the beneficiary state to offer to negotiate in good faith with the other riparians to reach appropriate agreements or arrangements. Paragraph 6(c) of BP 7.50, *supra* note 141, also suggests that the Bank could "urge the parties to resolve the issues through amicable means, such as consultations, negotiations, and good offices."

arise if the process were to be initiated and supervised by the unit which is responsible for the issues that need to be reviewed by the independent experts. Thus, the unit that initiated the project would play a minimal role in the independent experts' process, only providing information about the project under review. The experts are engaged and their terms of reference prepared jointly by these units. The experts are provided with the background information on the proposed project, as well as the assistance needed to complete their work efficiently.

The experts' terms of reference require that they examine the project details. If they deem it necessary to verify the project details or take any related action, the Bank makes its best efforts to assist. The experts meet on an *ad hoc* basis until they submit their report to the Bank, which may ask them to explain or clarify any aspect of their report.[221]

It is worth emphasizing that the experts have no decision-making role in the project's processing. Their technical opinion is submitted for the Bank's purposes only, and does not in any way determine the rights and obligations of the riparians.[222] Their opinion and conclusions are reviewed by these units, with a leading role for the Bank lawyers. This is, somehow, similar to the fact-finding process where the recommendations of the commission are not binding on the parties; the parties are only obliged to consider such recommendations in good faith. A number of observations can be made about this process.

First, the objecting riparian has no veto power over the project, and its objection does not prevent the Bank from financing the project. Similarly, the Watercourses Convention does not grant the notified state veto power over the proposed planned measures by the notifying state. Indeed, no international instrument grants the objecting state such veto power. The requirement for the consent of other riparians under the Madrid Declaration of 1911 was replaced by the requirement of consultation and negotiations by the Salzburg Resolution of 1961. In fact, the *Lake Lanoux Arbitration* had declared a few years before the Salzburg Resolution that consent of other riparians to the proposed project is neither a custom, nor a general principle of law.[223]

221 BP 7.50, para. 10.

222 BP 7.50, para. 11. It is noteworthy that Annex A to OMS 2.32, *supra* note 134, as well as Annex A to OD 7.50, *supra* note 140, were both entitled 'Technical Advice of Independent Experts'. However, paragraphs 8–11 of BP 7.50 are together entitled 'Seeking the Opinion of Independent Experts.' The change from 'advice' to 'opinion' is, in my view, intended to re-emphasize further that the experts have no decision-making role.

223 The Arbitral Tribunal, *supra* note 30, at 130, stated: "The rule according to which States may utilize the hydraulic force of international watercourses only on condition of a *prior*

Second, before starting the independent experts' process, the Policy suggests urging the parties to resolve the issues through amicable means such as consultations, negotiations, and good offices. This route will normally be resorted to when the other riparians' objections are substantiated because the Bank will not be able to finance the project if it is established that it will cause appreciable harm without the consent of the affected riparian or riparians. The Watercourses Convention follows a similar route with the process of the independent experts.

Third, the process of the independent experts involved a number of units within the Bank: the region where the project is being processed, the LEGVP which oversees the policy for projects on international waterways, and the Sustainable Development Network that deals with environment and natural resources. The latter is even required to maintain a roster of names for such experts. The involvement of those three units precludes conflict of interest situations, gives the process credibility and objectivity, and ensures its transparency and fairness.

Fourth, the issue of the possibility of conflict of interest is adequately addressed. The experts selected may not be nationals of any of the riparians of the waterways in question, and not just of the notifying and notified states. The experts may not have any other conflicts of interest in the matter. Similar provisions are included in the fact-finding process under the Watercourses Convention.

Fifth, the process is not an arbitration with binding decisions. On the contrary, the experts have no decision-making role in the project processing. Their technical opinion is submitted to the Bank, and the Bank decides what to do with it. Furthermore, their opinion does not in any way determine the rights and obligations of the riparians. Nonetheless, the Bank may ask them to explain or clarify any aspect of their report.[224] As stated earlier, the recommendations of the fact-finding Commission are not binding on the parties; such parties are only required to consider the recommendations in good faith.

Despite the overall similarities, the procedures established by the Bank are more elaborate than those proposed by the Watercourses Convention. This is understandable given the nature of the Bank as an international financial cooperative institution, with equal duties and responsibilities to all members, and indeed to all riparians.

---

agreement between the interested states cannot be established as a custom, or even less as a general principle of law."

224 BP 7.50, *supra* note 141, para. 10.

7.4 *Seeking Opinion of Independent Experts in Practice*

The Bank has received very few objections for the projects it has been financing on international waterways. The main reason for this situation is that the Bank ensures from the very beginning that its financed projects will not cause appreciable harm to any riparian. The purpose of the notification is basically to convey and confirm this fact about its projects to the other riparians, and obtain a reconfirmation to this effect from them. The notification letter and the accompanying project details often provide adequate information to this effect. In some instances, the notified riparians may ask for more information about the project, and the Bank ensures that such information is provided to them, with an emphasis that the project will not cause appreciable harm. This approach has resulted in very few of objections to Bank-financed projects on international waterways.

Furthermore, most of those objections stem from the poor relations between some of the riparian states themselves, rather than from matters related to the project. Issues not pertinent to the project such as the absence of notification by the beneficiary state to the other riparians of past projects not financed by the Bank, or failure of the borrower to become a party to a regional agreement on the shared watercourse, have been raised by some of the objecting riparians. The presence of other types of disputes, mainly border ones, has also been a frequent reason for objection to projects on the shared waterway.[225] The Bank has ruled generally that the objections to its financed projects did not have sufficient merit to warrant seeking the opinion of independent experts, as stipulated in its policies. Accordingly, the Bank proceeded with the processing of these projects without appointing independent experts to look into these objections.

One such a project was the Karakaya Hydropower Project in Turkey that the Bank started processing in the late 1970s on the Euphrates River which Turkey shares with Iraq and Syria.[226] The Project consisted of the construction of a hydropower plant with a reservoir and a 173-meter-high dam. The Bank notified both Syria and Iraq of the Project on behalf of Turkey, and provided them with the project details. As part of the preparation for the Project, Turkey confirmed its agreement with the 'Rule of 500' according to which Turkey would maintain a flow of no less than 500 cubic meters per second in the Euphrates at the Turkey-Syria border during the filling of the Karakaya reservoir.

225 This has been particularly true with regard to notification between Eritrea and Ethiopia before they resolved their border disputes in December 2018, as well as Armenia and Azerbaijan. *See* Salman, *The World Bank Policy*, *supra* note 86, at 152.

226 Turkey, Karakaya Hydropower Project (P008930, 1980).

However, despite the explicit inclusion of this Rule in the Project documents, Iraq objected to the Project, and insisted on the conclusion of an agreement on the equitable sharing of the waters of the river by the three riparians. Syria also objected to the project, and rejected the Rule of 500 claiming that this volume of water represented only over half the flow of the Euphrates to Syria, and demanded a more permanent and equitable arrangement. Following the objections from both Iraq and Syria to the Project,

> [t]he Bank assessed the objections from the two riparians and concluded that (i) it could rely on the formal representation of Turkey regarding the Rule of 500, which adequately protected the interests of Syria and Iraq, (ii) the consumptive use of the project would only last while the reservoir was being filled, and during that period the Rule of 500 would prevail,[227] and (iii) the Bank could only offer assistance for an agreement if all three riparians requested it; and, moreover, this matter was beyond the scope of the proposed project. Based on the above, the Bank decided to proceed with the project processing despite the objections by Iraq and Syria. The Loan Agreement for the project included a reference to the Rule of 500.[228] For these reasons the idea of appointing independent experts to look into the objections by Iraq and Syria was not considered by the Bank.[229]

Objection by one riparian state to the project when some of the other riparian states have responded positively, or have not respond at all, usually indicates the weak basis for the objection. As discussed above, in a number of instances such objection would be prompted by factors beyond the proposed project. Furthermore, when the relationship between two neighbours are not friendly, objections to projects on shared waterways are to be expected, but such objections are usually based on the general unfriendly relations, rather than on any adverse effects by the proposed project on the shared waterway and that particular riparian. More importantly, and as explained repeatedly, the Bank usually exerts an extra effort to ensure that the project would not cause

227 For more discussion of the Karakaya Project and the Rule of 500, *see* Kolars, *supra* note 99, at 44.

228 Preamble (B) to the Loan Agreement for the Project between the IBRD and Republic of Turkey stated that "[i]n order to safeguard adequately the interests of the lower riparian states, the Borrower will implement certain measures with respect to the construction, filling and operation of the dam included in the Project as set forth in the letters dated 7 March, 1979, and 22 February 1980, addressed to the Bank by the Borrower's Minister of Finance." Those letters included details on the Rule of 500.

229 Salman, *World Bank Policy*, *supra* note 86, at 152–153.

appreciable harm to any of the other riparians. For those reasons, appointment of independent experts to look into an objection by one of the riparians has been a very rare occasion.

The process of seeking the opinion of independent expert was put into effect for the first time in the history of the Bank in 1988 in the Baardhere Dam Project in Somalia.[230] The Project consisted of the construction of a multipurpose dam about 600 meters long and 75 meters high, to regulate the flow of the Juba River and to generate hydropower. The Project also included the construction of irrigation and drainage systems for about 5,000 hectares of land. The proposed Baardhere Dam was located on the Juba River, 35 kilometers upstream of the town Baardhere in Somalia. The Juba River is fed by three main tributaries: the Genale and the Wabe Gestro, which originate in Ethiopia, and the Dawa, which flows from Kenya. Those rivers converge at Dolo, near the Somali borders with Kenya and Ethiopia, forming the main Juba River. The River then flows through Somalia before emptying into the Indian Ocean.[231] Thus, Ethiopia is the upstream riparian and Somalia is the downstream riparian. Kenya is a riparian by virtue of the Dawa tributary that originates there. No agreement has been concluded on the River, nor have any basin management arrangements been established by the riparians for the River.

Processing of the Project started in 1983. In 1985, following adoption by the Bank of OMS 2.32 ‘Projects on International Waterways’, the Bank informed Somalia of the need to notify Ethiopia of the Project. However, because of the strained diplomatic relations between the two countries at that time, Somalia asked the Bank to undertake the notification on its behalf.

Consequently, the Bank notified the Government of Ethiopia of the proposed Baardhere Dam Project in September 1986. It provided information on the project basic design features to enable Ethiopia to make its own determination as to the likely impact of the Project, and stated that in the Bank's judgment, the Project would not cause appreciable harm to Ethiopia. Pursuant to the Bank policy, Ethiopia was asked to send any comments it might have within a period of six months, hence no later than March 1987.

In its reply of March 1987, the Ethiopian government took the position that Ethiopia had the potential to impound all the discharge of the Juba River for irrigation and hydropower development, and that the Project did not take into consideration present and future irrigation and hydropower developments within Ethiopia. Thus, Ethiopia's response also conveyed the concerns that

---

230 Somalia, Baardhere Dam Project (P002492, 1983).

231 For more details about the Juba River, *see* D. Caponera, *National and International Water Law and Administration: Selected Writings* (Kluwer Law International, 2003), at 221–222.

the Project would foreclose the potential for its future uses of the waters of the Juba River.[232] The Government of Ethiopia suggested prior negotiations with Somalia concerning the use of the waters of the Juba River, with the view of reaching an agreement that would be mutually satisfactory to both riparian states. Ethiopia went further and suggested negotiations with Somalia to determine the amount of water of the Juba River that each country would be allocated.

The Bank concluded that Ethiopia's reaction to the notification amounted to an objection to the proposed project. The Bank was also concerned that the future uses of Ethiopia could appreciably harm the Project. As a result, the Bank proposed that Somalia should hold negotiations with Ethiopia over the Juba River. At that stage, Kenya's role as a riparian was noted for the first time. Consequently, the Government of Somalia was advised of the need to notify Kenya of the proposed project. In response, Somalia asked the Bank to notify Kenya on its behalf, and this was done in November 1987. Kenya did not respond to the notification.

The Somali government was not amenable to the idea of negotiations with Ethiopia, or the use of good offices of a third party to facilitate a resolution of the issues raised by Ethiopia. Instead, Somalia proposed that the Bank should make its own assessment of Ethiopia's objection and claims. Ethiopia's proposal of negotiations conferred credibility on its objection, and made it difficult for the Bank to ignore it. Under these circumstances the question arose whether – for the first time – the matter should be referred to independent expert pursuant to paragraphs 11(e) and 13 of OMS 2.32 of 1985 and its Annex A 'Technical Advice of Independent Experts.'

After extensive internal deliberations, the Bank decided to proceed with appointment of independent experts. Three such experts were duly appointed in October 1988 after thorough and extensive preparations.[233] The terms of reference required the independent experts to (a) examine the nature of the riparian issues; (b) assess whether the proposed project would cause appreciable harm to other riparians, or would be harmed by the use of water by other riparians; and (c) give an opinion on the staff assessment of the riparian

232 Ethiopia's objection to the Baardhere Dam Project reflected its concerns that those waters would not be available in the future when Ethiopia became ready to use them. Thus, Ethiopia, the upstream riparian, claimed that the other downstream riparian, Somalia, can cause it harm. This position reflected Ethiopia's comprehension of the concept of foreclosure of future uses; *see supra* note 70. *See* also Salman, *supra* note 18.

233 The independent experts selected were Mr. Lloyd A. Duscha, Dr. Boonrod Binson (both engineers), and Dr. Dante Caponera (a water lawyer). Mr. Duscha was selected by the other two experts as the Chair of the group.

issues. Specifically, the experts would examine the project details and other project documents and studies, and as necessary take steps to verify Ethiopia's claims on past and proposed uses of the Juba River and its tributaries. The experts would also assess the viability of the project if water flow in the proposed Baardhere Dam is depleted, reduced, or altered by Ethiopia.[234] To ensure their independence, the experts were appointed and expected to report to the Senior Vice President, Operations; and not to the Vice President of the Africa Region where the project was being processed.[235] Their terms of reference included the possibility of field visits to Somalia, Ethiopia and Kenya.[236]

The independent experts met during the last week of May 1989, and submitted their report on 31 May 1989.[237] The report discussed both the technical issues associated with the project, as well as the basic principles of international water law.[238] The independent experts stated that the Baardhere Dam would cause no appreciable harm to Ethiopia or Kenya as the dam was downstream of both states and its reservoir limit was well within Somalia. It accepted as valid the analysis of the Bank staff that projected a 20 to 36 percent decrease in

---

234 Some discussion took place on whether the Bank should consult Ethiopia and Somalia on the terms of reference of the independent experts. However, it was decided that those were the Bank's independent experts, and hence there was no reason for the Bank to consult the parties.

235 Paragraph 2 of the Annex to OMS 2.32 of 1985 "Technical Advice of Independent Experts" stated that the Vice President, Operations Policy Staff "will, when so requested, select the experts from the roster in consultation with the Regional Office concerned and the Legal Department, to ensure the appropriate expertise and terms of reference. The experts should not be nationals of any of the riparians of the river or of other waterways involved and should have no conflict of interest in the matter."

236 Paragraph 10 of BP 7.50, *supra* note 141, states that if the experts "deem it necessary to verify the Project Details or take any related action, the Bank makes its best efforts to assist."

237 Report of Independent Experts on Riparian Issues – Somalia: Baardhere Dam Project, 23–31 May 1989, World Bank Headquarters, Washington, DC, submitted by Lloyd A. Duscha, Chairman, Dr. Boonrod Binson, Dr. Dante Caponera.

238 The independent experts cited a number of conventions and treaties of general relevance to the three riparian countries. They also cited the only treaty directly related to the Juba River, that is, the Treaty between the Empire of Ethiopia and the Republic of Kenya respecting the Boundary between the two Countries signed in Mombasa on 9 June 1970. The Treaty has no bearing on the Baardhere Dam. Article VII of the Treaty provides that with respect to the Dawa River between Malka Rie and Malka Marie, canalization of flood waters shall be permitted for cultivation, but no work shall be undertaken which might be prejudicial to the downstream water supply or which might alter the course of the river. Furthermore, the experts stated that both Ethiopia and Somalia are bound by the 1968 African Convention on the Conservation of Nature and Natural Resources (*supra* note 53) which requires prior consultation. For discussion of some of the legal aspects of the Report, *see* Caponera, *supra* note 231.

mean annual run-off due to abstractions and evaporations in Ethiopia.[239] The experts also noted that it was possible to decrease of the flow of the Juba River upstream of Somalia to the severe detriment of the project.

Equally important was the observation of the experts that the project could become a detriment to Ethiopia by virtue of prescriptive rights gained with time.[240] This point was mentioned again in connection with the general discussion of the principles of international water law. In that connection the experts observed that "present reasonable uses shall take into consideration the legitimate future requirements of a co-basin state which at present is not in a position to develop the same water resources in its territory."[241] The experts also underscored the principle of international water law of equitable and reasonable utilization of the waters of the Juba River among the three riparians, and thought that it was indispensable that negotiations between those riparians should take place with a view to concluding a framework agreement.[242]

The independent experts concluded that, considering the data available to it, the Bank staff had performed a reasonable and prudent analysis in developing its assessment, and that without direct knowledge of the actual situation or the future plans of Ethiopia particularly, the independent experts were in no position to dispute the conclusions reached by the Bank staff, which the experts deemed sound.[243] Accordingly, the independent experts confirmed the determination of the Bank that the project would not cause appreciable harm to the other riparians, and would not be harmed by other riparians possible water use. However, the experts qualified this conclusion by citing two factors, the data made available to them, and lack of direct knowledge of the actual situation in Ethiopia. Although the possibility of a field visit was included in the terms of reference, no such a visit took place.

---

239 The independent experts noted further that "[r]egardless of the true figure, it appears unlikely that development could be at a rate which would create a negative factor during the economic life of the project. It could however, become a factor during the physical life of the project." *See* Report of Independent Experts, *supra* note 237, at 2.

240 *Id.*, at 3.

241 *Id.*, at 8; *see also supra* note 18 on the concept of foreclosure of future uses.

242 The elements of a framework agreement were spelt out by the independent experts. They included establishment of an institutional mechanism, determination of priority actions on the river, a reciprocal acknowledgment of an equitable and reasonable utilization in the use of the Juba River, and more importantly, determination of a time limit after which the Baardhere Dam would be constructed.

243 For a detailed discussion of the Baardhere Dam and Infrastructure Project, the objection of Ethiopia, and the appointment and report of the independent experts, *see* S. M. A. Salman, *'The Baardhere Dam and Water Infrastructure Project in Somalia: Ethiopia's Objection and the World Bank Response'*, 56:4 Hydrological Sciences Journal (2011) 630–640.

In connection with the recommendation for a framework agreement, the independent experts proposed that they be permitted to visit the appropriate ministry heads in Ethiopia, Kenya, and Somalia to provide a vehicle for facilitation of negotiations between those riparians. This recommendation was clearly beyond their terms of reference and the role set forth for them under OMS 2.32, and thus there was no enthusiasm for it by the Bank staff. Indeed, the Bank staff were relieved and satisfied that their determination on the Project was vindicated by the Bank's first-ever appointed independent experts to review an objection to a Bank staff determination.

The independent experts were no doubt eminent authorities in their fields. It is worth noting that they represented both engineering and water law, the most relevant disciplines to the project and the objection. Clearly, the experts conducted their assignment in an independent environment, facilitated by the fact that they were selected by, and reported to, a unit other than the unit proposing the project.[244]

A few months after the report of the independent experts was submitted, the political and security situation in Somalia started to deteriorate, and as a result, the Bank suspended processing of the Project. Eventually, the situation in Somalia put an end to the processing of the Baardhere Dam Project. It would have been interesting to see how Ethiopia would have reacted to the decision of the Bank to proceed with the Project, and how the Bank would have addressed any further protests from Ethiopia.

The Baardhere Dam Project in Somalia was the first project that prompted the Bank to appoint independent experts to review an objection from one of the riparians to a project on an international waterway proposed for Bank financing. Despite the incomplete story, the Bank and the independent experts in the Baardhere Dam Project put in place, and implemented, an excellent road map for the selection and work of independent experts.

It can be argued that the process of the independent experts under the World Bank Policy for Projects on international waterways is not that different from the fact-finding commission process under the Watercourses Convention in the outcome and the extent it binds the parties.[245] As discussed above, the Convention states that if after six months from the time of the request for negotiations the parties concerned have not been able to settle their dispute through negotiation or other means, the dispute shall be submitted, at the request of any of the parties to the dispute, to an impartial fact-finding

244 See discussion of the process for the selection and work of the independent experts in part 7.4 of this monograph.

245 UN Watercourses Convention, supra note 62, art. 33, paras. 3–9.

commission. The parties concerned have the obligation to provide the commission with such information as it may require and, on request, to permit the commission to have access to their respective territory and to inspect any facilities, plant, equipment, construction, or natural feature relevant for the purpose of its inquiry. The report of the commission shall set forth its findings and the reasons therefore and such recommendations as it deems appropriate for an equitable solution of the dispute, which the parties concerned shall consider in good faith. This situation is similar to the obligation on the World Bank to consider the recommendations of the independent experts in good faith, although such recommendations are not binding on the Bank and do not determine the rights and obligations of the riparians.

7.5 *Objections by the Notified States and Existing Agreements*

One important issue that arose with regards to the manner in which the Bank would deal with an objection from one or more of the notified riparian states related to existing arrangements and agreements between the riparian themselves. Both the 1973 Treaty Concerning the Rio de la Plata[246] and the 1975 Statute of the River Uruguay[247] state that any dispute concerning the interpretation or application of either Treaty, which cannot be settled by direct negotiations, may be submitted by either of the parties to the International Court of Justice.[248] Similarly, the 1994 Danube Convention provides for the submission of any dispute arising between the parties to the ICJ or through arbitration, if the parties fail to resolve the dispute through negotiations with the assistance of the ICPDR.[249]

The Mahakali Treaty concluded between India and Nepal in 1996[250] refers any difference that may arise between the parties, as a first step, to the Mahakali River Commission. If either party disagrees with the recommendation of the Commission, then the difference becomes a dispute, and such a dispute would

246 *Supra* note 54.

247 *Id.*, and *supra* note 7.

248 1973 Treaty, *supra* note 54, para. 87; 1975 Treaty, *supra* note 7, para. 60.

249 Article 24 of the Danube Convention, *supra* note 162, lays down the situations for submission of a dispute to the ICJ. Annex V of Convention includes detailed provisions on arbitration.

250 Treaty Between His Majesty's Government of Nepal and the Government of India Concerning the Integrated Development of the Mahakali River Including Sarada Barrage, Tanakpur Barrage and Pancheshwar Project, 12 February 1996, 36 I.L.M. 531 (1997). For a general discussion of the Treaty, *see* S. M. A. Salman & K. Uprety, *'Hydro-Politics in South Asia: A Comparative Analysis of the Mahakali and the Ganges Treaties'*, 39 Natural Resources Journal (1999) 295–343; *see* also Salman and Uprety, *'Cooperation and Conflict'*, *supra* note 32 and *'Shared Watercourses'*, note 10.

be submitted for arbitration to a tribunal consisting of three arbitrators. Each party would appoint one arbitrator, and the third arbitrator, who would preside over the tribunal, would be appointed jointly. If the two parties fail to agree on the third arbitrator, either party may request the Secretary-General of the Permanent Court of Arbitration to appoint such arbitrator.[251]

The 1992 Agreement between Kazakhstan, the Kyrgyz Republic, Tajikistan, Turkmenistan, and Uzbekistan on cooperation in interstate water resources states that all disputes "have to be solved by the republican water-economic organizations heads, and if necessary, with participation of independent side's representative."[252] The Indus Waters Treaty establishes a unique system for resolving issues that may arise between the two parties. Questions regarding interpretation and application of the Treaty are referred to, and decided by the Permanent Indus Commission. Differences are dealt with by a neutral expert, and disputes by a court of arbitration.[253]

As discussed in this part of the monograph, the procedures that the Bank may follow in case of an objection from one or more of the riparians include the possibility of appointing independent experts. A question that could arise in this connection is: how would the Bank handle an objection from one of the riparians to a project on an international waterway that is governed by an agreement that includes its own provisions for dispute settlement? Will the Bank follow its own procedures or will it adhere to the procedures set forth in the agreement between the parties, such as those outlined above?

The situation may become more complicated if the objecting state invokes the provisions of a treaty and refers the dispute to the entity specified in that treaty for resolution, while the Bank is still reviewing and deciding how to handle the objection. Should the Bank abandon its independent experts process and decide to abide by the decision of this entity, or can it proceed with its own procedures for handling the objection, with the risk of two conflicting determinations?

The Bank has not yet faced any such situation. Objections to its financed projects have been few, and none of them confronted the Bank with the

251 Mahakali Treaty, *id.*, arts. 9 and 11. It is worth noting that the Mahakali Treaty uses the terms 'difference' and 'dispute' in the same manner used in the Indus Waters Treaty.

252 Agreement between the Republic of Kazakhstan, the Kyrgyz Republic, the Republic of Tajikistan, Turkmenistan and the Republic of Uzbekistan on Cooperation in the Field of Joint Management on Utilization and Protection of Water Resources from Interstate Sources, Alma-Ata, 18 February 1992, available at: http://www.icwc-aral.uz/legal_framework.htm, art. 13.

253 *See* Salman & Uprety, *Shared Watercourses*, *supra* note 10; *see also* Salman & Uprety, *Conflict and Cooperation*, *supra* note 32.

question of choice between its own procedures, and the procedures set forth in a treaty to which the borrower and the objecting riparian are parties. As discussed in part 5 of this monograph, the Bank policy for projects on international waterways requires the Bank to ascertain whether the riparians have entered into agreements or arrangements, or have established any institutional framework for the international waterway concerned.[254] It also requires confirmation if the issues involved are covered by an appropriate agreement or arrangement between the beneficiary state and the other riparians.[255]

It is worth emphasizing in this regard that the Bank policy for projects on international waterways does not supersede the riparians' obligations under any treaty or convention to which they are parties. Accordingly, the provisions on dispute settlement in any of those agreements would need to be carefully studied before a decision is taken on whether to follow the Bank's procedures on objection, or the procedures for dispute settlement set forth in that agreement. Any decision in this regard would have to be reached after consultations with the notifying and objecting riparians to avoid putting into effect concurrently two parallel processes for resolving the issues related to the objection of the notified state.

With regards to the Watercourses Convention, Article 3 states that in the absence of an agreement to the contrary, nothing in the present Convention shall affect the rights or obligations of a watercourse state arising from agreements in force for it on the date on which it became a party to the present Convention. Accordingly, the Convention establishes the supremacy of the agreement concluded by the parties concerned.

Moreover, the situation as to which rules would apply regarding an objection would get more interesting and complicated if the notifying and objecting riparians are also parties to the Watercourses Convention. Which rules would apply in this case? The arrangements concluded by the two riparian parties, the independent experts process under the Bank policy, or the fact-finding commission under the Watercourses Convention?

Thus, the Watercourses Convention and the Bank Policy approaches to objection from one or more of the riparians to the notification have the same objective of resolving the dispute amicably, without giving the objecting party veto power, and without giving the third party (fact finding commission or independent experts) judicial powers with binding decision. The recommendations of the fact-finding commission and the report and findings of the independent experts are merely an opinion to be considered in good faith.

254 OP 7.50, *supra* note 141, para. 5.

255 *Id.*, para. 8.

However, the provisions of the Convention are explicitly clearer with regards to the supremacy of the agreements concluded by the parties. As discussed before, the Bank Policy recognizes supremacy of existing agreements between riparian states over its Policy. However, any objection from one riparian state may still raise the question of whether to apply the Bank procedures, or those agreed by the parties, to deal with such an objection.

Part 8: Conclusion

The previous parts of this monograph have discussed in detail the major similarities and differences between the Watercourses Convention, and those enunciated in the World Bank policies and procedures and elaborated through the Bank practice, on the process of notification of other riparians of planned measures on shared watercourses. As discussed in part 3 of this monograph, the Watercourses Convention has, by and large, codified established principles of customary international water law, including those on notification. On the other hand, the Bank Policies have evolved as a result of the special status of the Bank as an international cooperative financial institution required under its Articles of Agreement to act prudently, in the interests both of the particular member in whose territory the project is located, as well as the members as a whole.

Actually, when the Bank was faced with the issues related to projects on shared watercourses, the Bank had to go beyond these parameters and take into consideration the interests of riparians who were not members of the Bank. The Bank lawyers pointed to the larger and more encompassing principles of international law that bind and protect the states of the world, whether they are members of the World Bank or not, and which the Bank ought to reflect in its policies and abide by.

Because of its nature as a cooperative financial institution, and to avoid disputes between the riparians on the one hand, and between the Bank and the other riparians on the other hand, the Bank chose to apply the strict requirement of notification without a threshold, believing that a threshold could trigger disputes. In that respect, the Bank relied on the decision of the *Lake Lanoux Arbitration*.[256]

Moreover, lack of international instruments dealing with the environment in the 1940s and 1950s, both at the global level and within the Bank, prompted the Bank to include in its policies both freshwater and semi-enclosed coastal

256 *Supra* note 30.

waters. The Bank even included national rivers flowing into semi-enclosed coastal waters. Because of this wider definition of the waters involved, the term 'waterways' was chosen over the term 'watercourses.' Furthermore, because the Bank was a financial institution whose mandate centres around funding of development projects, the Bank decided to list its funded projects that would be covered by its policies on projects on international waterways to avoid any ambiguity and disputes over the scope of application of the policy.

All in all, the Bank went through these developments, with little or no guidance because the field of international water law was in its infancy in the late 1940s and early 1950s when the Bank started financing projects affecting shared watercourses. Indeed, the Bank remained, and still remains, the only international institution with policies and extensive practical experience in the field of projects on shared watercourses.[257]

However, despite these differences, the Bank policies and practical experience with projects on shared watercourses, particularly with notification, have no doubt added an enormously rich literature to the field of international water law, and have influenced and been influenced by developments in this field. Indeed, the synergies between the detailed provisions on notification set forth in the Watercourses Convention, and the provisions of the World Bank successive policies and its vast practical experience, have enriched the field of notification considerably, addressed some complex situations, and filled major gaps, as shown throughout this monograph.

The Watercourses Convention requires a watercourse state, before it implements or permits the implementation of planned measures which may have a significant adverse effect upon other watercourse states, to provide those states with timely notification thereof. The Convention has used the term 'watercourses states' and not upstream and downstream riparians, thus mandating notification by and to all watercourse states. The Bank policies included, since its early days in the late 1940s, the same requirement of notification to all and by all riparians, regardless of their location on the shared watercourse. However, the Bank practice has clarified the rationale and reasons for notifying upstream riparians by downstream ones, and elucidated and abundantly clarified the concept of foreclosure of future uses, as discussed earlier.

257 The AIIB, *supra* note 23, adopted in March 2017 a series of operational policies, including the 'Operational Policy on International Relations'. Section 3 of the Operational Policy deals with international waterways. Although the AIIB also has a policy for projects on international waterways, the AIIB policy is quite recent, with no substantial implementation experience thus far.

As explained in detail throughout this monograph, upstream riparians can harm downstream ones through storage, diversion, and use of the waters of the shared rivers. Similarly, downstream riparians can also harm upstream riparians by foreclosing their future uses of the shared waters through the prior use of, and the claiming of rights to such water, and invoking the no harm obligation. A number of downstream riparians, and many Bank staff and managers, resisted this approach, and insisted that only upstream riparians can actually harm downstream ones. It took a long time and lots of efforts by the Bank experts in this field to convince those countries and staff, and to streamline and clarify this approach, not only in the Bank operations, but as a major principle of international water law.

This concept was taken a step further and explained and elaborated by the Bank, as well as by its highly qualified independent experts. This opportunity arose when an upstream riparian objected to a project in a downstream country, and the Bank accepted that objection and appointed independent experts to review and give an opinion thereon. That opinion addressed and endorsed the concept of foreclosure of future uses, thus solidifying the Bank approach in this regard.

Another area of synergy between the Watercourses Convention and the Bank policies and practice is the approach of indirect procedures to notification. The Watercourses Convention stipulates that in cases where there are serious obstacles to direct contacts between the watercourse states, the states concerned shall fulfil their obligations of cooperation provided for in the Convention, including exchange of data and information, notification, communication, consultations, and negotiations, through any indirect procedure accepted by them. The World Bank policies have included similar provisions through which the Bank would step in and undertake the notification on behalf of the prospective borrower (the beneficiary state of the project) if the borrower so requests the Bank, or has no objection to the Bank undertaking notification on its behalf. As is the case with the Watercourses Convention, this situation usually arises where there are serious obstacles to direct contacts between the watercourse states. The Bank Policy goes on and states that if the prospective borrower does not wish to give notification, and objects to the Bank's doing so, the Bank discontinues processing of the project. Thus, the Bank has made it clear that notification is a basic requirement under its policies as well as under international water law and cannot be overlooked or bypassed.

Both the Watercourses Convention and the Bank Policy reflect established customary international water law in this regard, with each contributing to the evolution and progressive development of the other. Although it may be argued that the Bank Policy is more strict than the provisions of the Convention as it establishes no threshold for notification, it can also be argued that the exceptions to the notification requirement under the Bank Policy would erode this stipulation.

It should be added that the practical experience of the World Bank has shown innovative approaches for undertaking notification, such as through the use of river basin management organizations if the establishing instruments of the organizations allow such a role. Moreover, the Bank has taken the role of the river basin management organizations many steps forward by accepting the response of the organization to the notification on the effects of the project on behalf of the members of the organization, if the agreement establishing the organization endows the organization with this authority. Such an approach has taken place in number of cases, including the Niger Basin Authority, the Lake Chad Basin Commission, and the Danube Commission, all of which have the authority to respond on behalf of the respective riparians. This is, no doubt, a major addition to the notification requirement and to international water law.

Indeed, the Bank has gone a step further and allowed river basin management organizations to play a role in the notification process even if the establishing instrument is silent on this issue, if all the members of such an organization request or agree to such approach. The Bank followed a similar approach with the Nile Basin Initiative (NBI) Secretariat, which would act in such cases on behalf of the borrower, and send the notification to all the other riparians, and ask for any responses they may have. The NBI Secretariat would compile such responses and send them the World Bank, and would coordinate its actions during the notification process with the borrower, as well as with the Bank. The Bank has accepted and allowed this arrangement although the instrument establishing the NBI does not explicitly grant it such powers. This has resolved the problem of notification in the Nile Basin which, as discussed in part 1 of this monograph, is a very delicate and complex issue, and is still a pending issue in the way of final agreement on the Nile Basin Cooperative Framework Agreement. It has also helped in dispute avoidance, and in strengthening the NBI Secretariat. Indeed, this method for notification has resulted in the innovative approach of notification through the International Panel of Experts for the Grand Ethiopian Renaissance Dam.

The Bank has also used some United Nations organs to assist with notification for territories under the administration of the United Nations, as happened in Kosovo and Namibia when both were under UN administration. In the case of Kosovo, the Bank decided that for projects on shared watercourses, the United Nations Mission in Kosovo would be approached and asked to undertake the notification on behalf of Kosovo.

A similar approach was followed for the Lesotho Highlands Water Project which was processed by the World Bank when Namibia was still under the administration of the United Nations Council for South West Africa (Namibia) (UN Council). The Bank decided to send the notification to the UN Council which was then the legal administering authority of Namibia, and the UN Council voiced no objection to the project. Lesotho was also asked to consult with the South West Africa People's Organization (SWAPO) which was recognized by the UN as the representative of the people of Namibia. SWAPO also had no objection to the Project. This approach has helped in avoiding future disputes, and has been a major addition to the literature on notification, as well as to international water law.

With regards to the possible responses to notification, the Watercourses Convention and the Bank policies (including the Bank Good Practice) together list five such possible responses: consent or no objection; absence of reply; request for additional time; request for additional information; and objection to the planned measure. However, the practical experience of the Bank has added some flesh to the bones of these generalizations and elaborated them considerably. Furthermore, the Bank experience has included more possible responses such as 'qualified no objection', or even 'conditional no-objection.' These types of responses have forced the thinking of how to classify and deal with them, thus energizing and enriching the discussion on notification, as well as on objections to such notification.

Major synergies can also be discerned between the Watercourses Convention and the Bank policy and practice with regards to how to handle an objection to the planned measure by one or more of the riparian states. Both the Watercourses Convention and the Bank policies and practice have made it clear that the objecting state or states have no veto power over the project. Both have laid down detailed procedures for dealing with such an objection. The Watercourses Convention requires the parties to enter into good faith consultations and negotiations with a view of arriving at an equitable resolution of the situation that would take into account the two basic principles of international water law: equitable and reasonable utilization and the obligation not to cause harm. The fact-finding commission under Article 33 of the Convention could be invoked to assist with resolution of the dispute, if the dispute persists.

The Bank policies and practical experience have, similarly, laid down a detailed road map for dealing with any such objections. This road map includes the possibility, ultimately, of the appointment of independent experts to review the objection and submit an opinion thereon on the Bank. Such experts would play a substantial role in the settlement of the dispute over the proposed project. However, the Bank policy hastens to clarify that the independent experts have no decision-making role in the project processing, and their technical opinion is submitted for the Bank's purposes only, and does not in any way determine the rights and obligations of the parties. The Bank will decide what to do with the opinion of the independent experts. Similarly, the Watercourses Convention states that the fact-finding Commission shall submit its report to the parties concerned, setting forth its findings and the reasons therefor, and such recommendations as it deems appropriate for an equitable resolution to the dispute, which the parties concerned shall consider in good faith. Thus, neither the technical opinion of the independent experts under the Bank policy, nor the recommendations of the fact-finding Commission under the Watercourses Convention have a legally binding effect. Nonetheless, it is difficult to think that the Bank will not consider such opinion in good faith, as well, being in line with the requirements of the Watercourses Convention.

The subject of the environmental impact assessment for the planned measures on shared watercourses is another area for synergy between the Watercourses Convention and the World Bank policies and practice. The Convention, as discussed in part 3 of this monograph, does not mandate the carrying out of an EIA for the planned measures that are the subject of notification. Article 12 states: "Such notification shall be accompanied by available technical data and information including the results of any environmental impact assessment, to enable the notified States to evaluate the possible effects of the planned measures." Thus, the Convention is only suggestive of the carrying out of an EIA for the planned measures.

On the other hand, the Bank has taken, since the late 1990s, a very firm stance on the need to prepare and disclose to the public, the EIA for any project it proposes to finance. This approach was dictated, and further strengthened, by adoption of the safeguard policies, including the policy on disclosure of information. As a result, the project details furnished to the notified states by the prospective borrower or by the Bank would, by necessity, include the results of the EIA, and the link to such an EIA in the World Bank website. In fact, a number of the requests for additional information and time from the notified riparians to the notifying state or to the Bank revolve around the EIA, or the time needed to study it.

The Bank approach on the mandatory nature of the EIA has prevailed. As discussed in the preceding parts of this monograph, the ICJ endorsed and confirmed in the *Pulp Mills* case the need for an EIA. In that case, the ICJ stated explicitly that the Court considered it a requirement under general international law to undertake an EIA where there is a risk that the proposed industrial activity may have a significant adverse impact in a transboundary context, in particular, on a shared resource.[258] Thus, the ICJ has clearly endorsed the Bank's practice.

Another area of major synergy between the Watercourses Convention and the Bank policies and practice can be found in the manner transboundary groundwater is being dealt with. As discussed earlier, the Watercourses Convention defines the term 'international watercourses' to include groundwater connected to surface water only, and thus excludes shared fossil aquifers that have no connections to surface water. This has raised the question as to whether notification is really not required under the Convention for projects affecting shared fossil aquifers. Few experts, if any, would take and argue that approach. Accordingly, there is almost a consensus that there is a large lacuna in the Convention in this area, which does not reflect fully the basic principles of international water law.[259]

Although the successive Bank policies have not included any explicit reference to transboundary groundwater, the practice of the Bank since 1991 has been to include all types of transboundary groundwater in the definition of international waterways and to require notification of all the states sharing such bodies of groundwater. It is interesting to note that the first two projects that prompted the Bank to include shared aquifers in the definition of international waterways related to fossil aquifers, the very same type of aquifers that the Watercourses Convention has not included in the definition of international watercourses.

---

258 *Supra* note 6, para. 204.

259 As discussed above (*supra* note 131), after the ILC completed its work on the Watercourses Convention in 1994, it passed a resolution recommending treatment of all types of aquifers in the manner elaborated in the Convention. For more analysis of this matter and discussion of the resolution, *see* Krishna & Salman, *supra* note 145. This is exactly what the World Bank has been doing since 1991, namely, treating all types of shared aquifers as international waterways under its policies, requiring notification of other states sharing that aquifer. This position by the Bank underscores the close inter-connections and synergies between the Watercourses Convention and the Bank policies and practice with regards to transboundary groundwater. The approach of treating all types of aquifers in the same way was finally adopted by the ILC on 5 August 2008 when it concluded the work on the Draft Articles on the Law of Transboundary Aquifers, and submitted the Draft Articles to the United Nations General Assembly. Notification for planned activities that may affect a transboundary aquifer is addressed in Article 15 of the Draft Articles, which is based largely on the corresponding articles of the Watercourses Convention. For a more detailed discussion of the Draft Articles and their current status, *see* G. Eckstein, *The International Law of Transboundary Groundwater Resources*, *supra* note 148.

This is no doubt a major synergy between the Convention and the Bank practice. The on-going global attempts to cover all types of shared aquifers (whether replenishable or fossil) with the same protection, and rights and obligations to the riparians sharing it, will no doubt benefit and make use of the Bank experience in this field. Covering all types of shared aquifers is already becoming the globally accepted requirement under international water law.

Thus, it can be concluded that the provisions of the Watercourses Convention on notification and the World Bank policies and practical experience possess major and substantial synergies and fill some major gaps when riparians are confronted with issues not explicitly covered by either instrument. Riparian states, other international and regional financial institutions, as well as river basin management organizations can, and indeed should, utilize these synergies to streamline and standardize the notification process for projects on shared watercourses. This will no doubt be a major building block for enhancing cooperation in the field of shared watercourses.

Indeed, cooperation is the *sine qua non* for the management, sharing, and protection of shared watercourses. As a matter of fact, international water law is termed as the law of cooperation. The Watercourses Convention underscores the need for cooperation in the preamble as well as in the different provisions of the Convention itself. Article 8 is titled "General Obligation to Cooperate", and requires the riparian states to cooperate on the basis of sovereign equality, territorial integrity, mutual benefit, and good faith in order to attain optimal utilization and adequate protection of an international watercourse.

Similarly, the Bank Policy recognizes that cooperation and goodwill of riparians is essential for the efficient use and protection of the waterway. The Policy emphasizes that the Bank attaches great importance to riparians' making appropriate agreements or arrangements for these purposes for the entire waterway or any part thereof. The Policy goes on to state that the Bank stands ready to assist riparians in achieving this end.

Notification of the other riparians of planned measures and projects on the shared watercourse by the state planning such measures or projects is one important component and reflection of cooperation. Not only would notification help in avoiding future disputes between the riparians, it can also pave the way for discussing and negotiating the optimal ways for protecting and utilizing the shared watercourse. Notification, and the likely resulting cooperation, can also help in the establishment of an *ad hoc*, or even a permanent, river basin management organization for overseeing the sharing and management of the shared watercourse. This can end the current inefficient unilateral development plans and projects (which necessitate notification in the first place), and can also lead to the adoption of joint projects and programs for the shared watercourse by its riparian states. Such joint projects and programs would, by necessity, and as a result, put an end to the need for the lengthy and inherently dispute-ridden process of notification, and the likely resulting objection by one or more of the riparian states to the shared watercourse.

Thus, if followed and adopted in good faith and in the spirit of cooperation, notification could pave the way and result in more cooperation, reflected in joint projects and programs, as well as in the establishment of basin management organizations for the shared watercourse. This would, in turn, lead to the ultimate optimal and more efficient utilization and protection of shared watercourses.

Author Biography

Dr. Salman M. A. Salman
is the Editor-in-Chief of *Brill Research Perspectives in International Water Law* journal, and a Fellow with the International Water Resources Association (IWRA). Until 2009, he served as the World Bank Adviser on Water Law. Prior to that, he worked as a Legal Officer with the International Fund for Agricultural Development of the United Nations (IFAD) in Rome, Italy, and taught law at the University of Khartoum in Sudan. Dr Salman is the co-recipient of the IWRA Crystal Drop Award 2017, and has published extensively on issues related to water law and policy. Most of his writings are available at: www.salmanmasalman.org.

Bibliography

Alam, U. Z., *'Water Rationality: Mediating the Indus Waters Treaty'* (Unpublished Ph.D. Thesis, University of Durham, United Kingdom, 1998).

Black, E. R., *'The Indus: A Moral for Nations'*, *The New York Times* (11 December 1960).

Boisson de Chazournes, L., et al (eds.), *The UN Convention on the Law of the Non-Navigational Uses of International Watercourse: A Commentary* (Oxford: Oxford University Press, 2018).

Boisson de Chazournes, L., *Freshwater and International Law: The Interplay between Universal, Regional and Basin Perspectives* (Paris: UNESCO, 2009).

Boisson de Chazournes, L., & K. Sangbana, *'Principle 19: Notification and Consultation on Activities with Transboundary Impact'*, in J. E. Viñuales (ed.), *The Rio Declaration on Environment and Development: A Commentary* (Oxford: Oxford University Press, 2015) 493–507.

Bogdanovic, S., *International Law of Water Resources: Contribution of the International Law Association* (Kluwer Law International, 2001).

Bogdanovic, S., *'The International Law Association Helsinki Rules – Contribution to International Water Law'*, 3:4 International Water Law (2018).

Bourne, C., *'The International Law Association's Contribution to International Water Resources Law'*, 36 Natural Resources Journal (1996) 155–216.

Browder, G. & L. Ortolano, *'The Evolution of an International Water Resources Management Regime in the Mekong River Basin'*, 40:3 Natural Resources Journal (2000) 499–531.

Caponera, D., *National and International Water Law and Administration: Selected Writings* (Kluwer Law International, 2003).

Crow, B., *Sharing the Ganges: The Politics and Technology of River Development* (New Delhi: Sage Publications, 1995).

del Castillo-Laborde, L., *The Río de la Plata and its Maritime Front Legal Regime* (Leiden/Boston: Martinus Nijhoff Publishers, 2008).

Dubicki, A., & A. Nalberczynski, *'Development of the International Cooperation in the Oder River Basin'*, in M. Landsberg-Uczciwek, M. Adriaanse & R. Enderlein (eds.), *Management of Transboundary Waters in Europe* (Poland, 1998).

Eckstein, G., *The International Law of Transboundary Groundwater Resources* (Routledge, 2017).

Eckstein, G., *'A Hydrological Perspective of the Status of Ground Water Resources Under the UN Watercourse Convention'*, 30 Columbia Journal of Environmental Law (2005) 525–564.

Farrajota, M. M., *'Notification and Consultation in the Law Applicable to International Watercourses'*, in L. Boisson de Chazournes & S. M. A. Salman (eds.), *Water Resources and International Law* (The Hague Academy of International Law, 2005) 281–339.

Food and Agriculture Organization (FAO), *Treaties Concerning the Non-Navigational Uses of International Watercourses – Africa*, FAO Legislative Study 61 (Rome: FAO, 1997).

Godana, B. A., *Africa's Shared Water Resources, Legal and Institutional Aspects of the Nile, Niger and Senegal River* Systems (Francis Pinter Publishers, 1985).

International Bank for Reconstruction and Development, *Eleventh Annual Report 1955–1956* (Washington, DC: The World Bank, 1956).

International Bank for Reconstruction and Development and International Development Association, *1965–1966 Annual Report* (Washington, DC: The World Bank, 1966).

International Court of Justice, *Case concerning Pulp Mills on the River Uruguay (Argentina v. Uruguay)*, Judgement, 20 April 2010.

International Panel of Experts, *Grand Ethiopian Renaissance Dam: Final Report* (Addis Ababa, 31 May 2013).

Kinna, R. & A. Rieu-Clarke, *'The Governance Regime of the Mekong River Basin: Can the Global Water Conventions Strengthen the 1995 Mekong Agreement?'*, 2:1 International Water Law (2017).

Kirmani, S. & G. Le Moigne, *'Fostering Riparian Cooperation in International River Basins, The World Bank at its Best in Development Diplomacy'*, World Bank Technical Paper No. 335 (Washington, DC: The World Bank, 1997).

Kolars, J., *'Problems of International River Management: The Case of the Euphrates'*, in A. K. Biswas (ed.), *International Waters of the Middle East: From Euphrates-Tigris to Nile* (Oxford University Press, 1994) 45–94.

Krishna, R., *'Evolution and Context of the Bank Policy for Projects on International Waterways'*, in S. M. A. Salman & L. Boisson de Chazournes, *International Watercourses – Enhancing Cooperation and Managing Conflict*, World Bank Technical Paper No. 414 (Washington, DC: The World Bank, 1998) 31–43.

Krishna, R., *'International Watercourses: World Bank Experience and Policy'*, in J. A. Allan & C. Mallat (eds.), *Water in the Middle East: Legal, Political and Commercial Implications* (I. B. Tauris Publishers, 1995).

Krishna, R., *International Waters in Bank Projects: History and Case Studies*, Legal Department Working Paper No. 2 (Washington, DC: The World Bank, 1973).

Krishna, R., & S. M. A. Salman, *'International Groundwater Law and the World Bank Policy for Projects on Transboundary Groundwater'*, in S. M. A. Salman (ed.), *Groundwater: Legal and Policy Perspectives*, World Bank Technical Paper No. 456 (Washington, DC: World Bank, 1999) 163–189.

Lake Lanoux Arbitration (France v. Spain), 24 I.L.R. 101 (1957).

Landsberg-Uczciwek, M., M. Adriaanse & R. Enderlein (eds.), *Management of Transboundary Waters in Europe* (Poland, 1998).

Leb, C., *Cooperation in the Law of Transboundary Water Resources* (Cambridge: Cambridge University Press, 2013).

Lipper, J., *'Equitable Utilization,'* in A. H. Garretson et al (eds.), *The Law of International Drainage Basins* (Dobbs Ferry, NY: Oceana Publications, 1967) 16–26.

MacChesney, B., *'Lake Lanoux Case (France-Spain)'*, 53:1 American Journal of International Law (1959) 156–171.

Macoun, A., & H. El Naser, *'Groundwater Resources Management in Jordan: Policy and Regulatory Issues'*, in S. M. A. Salman (ed.), *Groundwater: Legal and Policy Perspectives*, World Bank Technical Paper No. 456 (Washington, DC: World Bank, 1999) 105–115.

Mason, E., & R. Asher, *The World Bank Since Bretton Woods* (Washington, DC: Brookings Institution, 1973).

McCaffrey, S., *The Law of International Watercourses: Non-Navigational Uses* (Oxford: Oxford University Press, 2nd ed., 2007).

McCaffrey, S., *'Water Disputes Defined: Characteristics and Trends for Resolving Them'*, in International Bureau, Permanent Court of Arbitration, ed., *Resolution of International Water Disputes* (The Hague/London/New York: Kluwer Law International, 2003) 49–90.

McCaffrey, S., C. Leb, & R. T. Denoon (eds.), *Research Handbook on International Water Law* (Cheltenham: Edward Elgar, 2019).

Mekonnen, D., *'The Nile Basin Cooperative Framework Agreement Negotiations and the Adoption of a "Water Security" Paradigm: Flight into Obscurity or a Logical Cul-de-sac?'*, 21:2 European Journal of International Law (2010) 421–440.

Odili, N. C., *'Shared Water Resources in West Africa – Relevance and Application of the UN Watercourses and the UNECE Water Conventions'*, 3:1 International Water Law (2018).

Paisley, R., et al, *'Transboundary Waters, Infrastructure Development, and Public Private Partnership: Through the Prism of the Nam Theun 2 and Xayaburi Hydropower Projects'*, 2:4 International Water Law (2017).

Rieu-Clarke, A., *'Notification and Consultation Procedures Under the Mekong Agreement: Insights From the Xayaburi Controversy'*, 5:1 Asian Journal of International Law (2015) 143–175.

Rosenstock, R., *'Second Report on the Law of the Non-navigational Uses of International Watercourses by Mr. Robert Rovenstock, Special Rapporteur'*, II (2) Yearbook of International Law Commission (1994) 88–135.

Salman, S. M. A., *'The Nile River Basin and its Changing Legal Contours'*, in S. McCaffrey, C. Leb & R. T. Denoon (eds.), *Research Handbook on International Water Law* (Cheltenham: Edward Elgar, 2019) 379–396.

Salman, S. M. A., *'The Obligation not to Cause Significant Harm'*, in Boisson de Chazournes et al (eds.), *The United Nations Convention on the Law of the Non-Navigational Uses of International Watercourse: A Commentary* (Oxford: Oxford University Press, 2018) 95–122.

Salman, S. M. A., *'The Nile Basin Cooperative Framework Agreement: The Impasse is Breakable!'*, available at: https://www.internationalwaterlaw.org/blog/2017/06/19/the-nile-basin-cooperative-framework-agreement-the-impasse-is-breakable/.

Salman, S. M. A., *'The Grand Ethiopian Renaissance Dam: The Road to the Declaration of Principles and the Khartoum Document'*, 41:4 Water International (2016) 512–527.

Salman, S. M. A., *'Entry into Force of the UN Watercourses Convention: Why Should It Matter?'*, 31:1 International Journal of Water Resources Development (2015) 4–16.

Salman, S. M. A., *'The Nile Basin Cooperative Framework Agreement: A Peacefully Unfolding African Spring?'*, 38:1 Water International (2013) 17–29.

Salman, S. M. A., *'The Baardhere Dam and Water Infrastructure Project in Somalia: Ethiopia's Objection and the World Bank Response'*, 56:4 Hydrological Sciences Journal (2011) 630–640.

Salman, S. M. A., *'The New State of South Sudan and the Hydro-politics of the Nile Basin'*, 36:2 Water International (2011) 154–166.

Salman, S. M. A., *'Downstream Riparians Can also Harm Upstream Riparians: The Concept of Foreclosure of Future Uses'*, 35:4 Water International (2010) 350–364.

Salman, S. M. A., *The World Bank Policy for Projects on International Waterways: An Historical and Legal Analysis* (Leiden: Martinus Nijhoff Publishers, 2009; Washington, DC: World Bank, 2009).

Salman, S. M. A. (ed.), *'Groundwater: Legal and Policy Perspectives'*, World Bank Technical Paper No. 456 (Washington, DC: World Bank, 1999).

Salman, S. M. A., & K. Uprety, *'Shared Watercourses and Water Security in South Asia – Challenges of Negotiating and Enforcing Treaties'*, 3:3 International Water Law (2018).

Salman, S. M. A., & K. Uprety, *Conflict and Cooperation on South Asia's International Rivers: A Legal Perspective* (The Hague: Kluwer Law International, 2003; Washington, DC: World Bank, 2003).

Salman, S. M. A., & K. Uprety, *'Hydro-Politics in South Asia: A Comparative Analysis of the Mahakali and the Ganges Treaties'*, 39 Natural Resources Journal (1999) 295–343.

Sangbana, K., *'Notification and Consultation Concerning Planned Measures'*, in Boisson de Chazournes et al (eds.), *The UN Convention on the Law of the Non-Navigational Uses of International Watercourses: A Commentary* (Oxford: Oxford University Press, 2018).

Schwebel, S., *'Third Report on the Law of the Non-navigational Uses of International Watercourses'*, II (1) Yearbook of the International Law Commission (1982), UN Doc. A/CN.4/348 and Corr. 1, 65–191.

Shapland, G., *Rivers of Discourse, International Water Disputes in the Middle East* (London: Hurst & Company, 1997).

Tanzi, A., & M. Arcari, *The United Nations Convention on the Law of International Watercourses* (The Hague: Kluwer, 2001).

Trail Smelter Arbitration (United States v. Canada), 3 R.I.A.A. 1911 (1941).

Waterbury, J., *The Nile Basin: National Determinants of Collective Action* (Yale University Press, 2002).

World Bank, *The World Bank Environmental and Social Framework* (Washington, DC: The World Bank, 2017).

World Bank, *Making the Most of Scarcity, Accountability for Better Water Management in the Middle East and North Africa* (Washington, DC: The World Bank, 2007).

World Bank, *From Scarcity to Security: Averting a Water Crisis in the Middle East and North Africa* (Washington, DC: The World Bank, 1998).

World Bank, *Riparian Rights: The Bank Experience: Staff Review and Recommendations* (Washington, DC: The World Bank, 1985).

Wouters, P. (ed.), *International Water Law: Selected Writings of Professor Charles B. Bourne* (London: Kluwer Law International, 1997).

Yihdego, Z., '*The Fairness Dilemma in Sharing the Nile Waters: What Lessons from the Grand Ethiopian Renaissance Dam?*', 2:2 International Water Law (2017).
Yihdego, Z., A. Rieu-Clarke & A. Elisa Cascao (eds.), *The Grand Ethiopian Renaissance Dam and the Nile Basin – Implications for Transboundary Water Cooperation* (Routledge, London 2018).

www.ingramcontent.com/pod-product-compliance
Lightning Source LLC
Chambersburg PA
CBHW031329230926
51848CB00001B/152
9789004407442